Edward M. Estabrooke

The ferrotype, and how to make it

Edward M. Estabrooke

The ferrotype, and how to make it

ISBN/EAN: 9783742827203

Manufactured in Europe, USA, Canada, Australia, Japa

Cover: Foto ©Andreas Hilbeck / pixelio.de

Manufactured and distributed by brebook publishing software (www.brebook.com)

Edward M. Estabrooke

The ferrotype, and how to make it

THE
FERROTYPE,
AND
HOW TO MAKE IT.

BY

EDWARD M. ESTABROOKE.

NINTH EDITION.

E. & H. T. ANTHONY & CO.,
NEW YORK.
1894.

CONTENTS.

CHAPTER I—POSITIVE PHOTOGRAPHY, . . . 11-22
  Definition of Term—Characteristics of Positive Pictures—Reasons for Popularity of the Ferrotype—Brief History of Photography.

CHAPTER II—THE FERROTYPE, . . . 23-25
  Its Superiority over all other Positive Pictures.

CHAPTER III—THE FERROTYPE GALLERY, . . . 26-28

CHAPTER IV—THE GLASS ROOM, ... 28-51
  List of Requisites of Glass Room—Construction of Glass Room—Top Light, effect of—Side Light—Advantages of Combined Top and Side Light—Devices to Exclude Sunlight—Best Method of Shading Light—The Camera Stand—Camera Boxes—Care of Plate-holder—Posing Chair—Head Rests—Curtain Supports—Copying Stand—Table and Table Cover—Ottomans—Finishing Stand—Varnish.

CHAPTER V—THE DARK ROOM, . . . 51-55
  Its Contents—Construction of the Sink.

CHAPTER VI—COLLODION, ... 55-62
  How to Prepare Gun Cotton—Proper Solvents for Gun Cotton—Direction for Selection of Ether and Alcohol—Excitants—Choice of Excitants—Bingham's Formula for Double Iodides and

(iii)

CONTENTS.

Bromides—Bingham's Collodion—Formulas for Standard Ferrotype Collodion—Preservation and Restoration of Collodion—Harmony of Bath and Collodion—Flowing Collodion.

CHAPTER VII—SILVER, ... 80-85

Historical Account of Metallic Silver—Nitrate of Silver—How to Prepare—Precipitation and Reduction of Nitrate of Silver—Preparation of a Silver Solution—Disturbing Elements of Silver Solution—Free Iodide—How to Restore an Old Bath—Saving of Silver Wastes—Bath Dishes.

CHAPTER VIII—DEVELOPER AND DEVELOPMENT, . 86-100

Protosulphite of Iron—Its Action upon Nitrate of Silver—Various Acids Used in Developer—Acetic Acid—Production of—Its Use—Alcohol and Its Use in Development—Essential Qualities—Formula for Developer—Importance of the Study of Development—Fixing Solution.

CHAPTER IX—THE COLLODION PROCESS, . . 101-113

Coating Plates—Exposure—Development—Fixing—Drying—Finishing.

CHAPTER X—FOG, AND OTHER CAUSES OF FAILURE, 114-122

Necessity of Adoption of Processes Recommended—Important Trio of Essential Parts in Collodion Process—Impurity of Chemicals—Fog—Comets—Free Iodide—Perpendicular Lines—Horizontal Lines—Crapy Appearance of Film—White Spots—Fan-shaped Marks—Slipping of the Film—Scum—Oily Spots or Lines—Stains—Finger Marks—Necessity of Cleanliness.

CHAPTER XI—COMPOSITION AND ILLUMINATION, 123-44

General Ignorance of the Subject—Responsibility of the Operator—Necessity for Pictorial Effect—

CONTENTS.

Art as Applied to Photography—Posing—Position of Camera—Draperies—Subserviency of Accessories to Likeness—Directions for Handling Sitters—Illumination—Effects of Different Lights—Top Light—Side Light—Top and Side Lights Combined—Examples—Composition of Groups.

CHAPTER XII—VIGNETTES, MEDALLIONS, ETC., . 141-142
Original Methods of Making Vignettes—Method now in Use—Description of Vignettes—Medallion Ferrotype, How to Make.

NON-REVERSED FERROTYPES, ... 158-160

THE NON-REVERSED MEDALLION FERROTYPE, 161-163

ADDENDA—WEIGHTS AND MEASURES, ... 164-167
Table of Enlargements—Thermometer Scales—Formula to Remove Silver Stains—Sizes of Camera Plates

PUBLISHERS' PREFACE.

We do not feel that we have any apology to make to the profession for the publication of this work; on the contrary, our only regret is that we did not undertake it a year or two ago. For the past ten years, so much attention has been given to the Photograph, that the merits of the Ferrotype have been ignored as far as possible. Books have been issued one after another devoted to the negative, and printing and toning; and cameras, printing frames, and apparatus have been constructed especially to aid in producing the paper picture. Nearly all effort and thought has run in this one direction.

About three years ago we observed many signs of dissatisfaction with the Photograph. In spite of all declarations that it would not fade, nearly all that were made for the public soon lost their value as a likeness or a work of art. The people began to want something better and more permanent, and we found in our orders a strong and increasing demand for Ferrotype goods. Manufacturers of apparatus found it was for their interest to improve the Multiplying Camera. New styles and designs of mounting cards have been introduced. Dealers have found it difficult to keep sufficient stock to supply the demand. As an evidence of the amount now in use, we received at one house, but a short time ago, nearly two tons of plates in one shipment, and we are selling at this time about as many goods for the Ferrotype as for the Photograph.

With such a state of affairs, it is apparent to all that a book of instruction on this subject is greatly needed, and we claim to be the first who proposed publishing such a work. Since it has been announced, we have received so many orders from all parts of the continent, that we are more than ever satisfied of the wisdom of its publication.

One word about the delay in its appearance. Our author, Mr. Estabrooke, was not willing the book should be issued until he had thoroughly worked up the subject in all its bearings. There was a good deal of unavoidable delay in getting the early history as complete as we desired it. Mr. V. M. Griswold, who was preparing an account of his invention and introduction of the Ferro-plate for this work, was taken sick and died after a short illness, when it was nearly completed. We regard the items he contributed as adding greatly to the value of this work, and believe all will rejoice that the information he possessed has been saved. Other parties, who were able to give us interesting incidents delayed their answers, so that it is the historical part which has hindered us. This has given the author better opportunities to arrange and collate his facts and instruction, and we are confident the value of the book is much increased by the delay. We hope it may greatly aid and improve the production of the beautiful and enduring Ferrotype.

THE PUBLISHERS.

PUBLISHERS' PREFACE
TO THE FOURTH EDITION.

The former editions of this work having been exhausted, the undersigned, into whose possession the copyright has fallen, have thought it desirable, in view of the extent to which the Ferrotype is used, to issue a fourth edition, which will be improved to the reader by means of a concluding chapter, wherein any improvements in the art of making ferrotypes will be detailed. Some remarks in reference to matters alluded to in former editions, which, in consequence of lapse of time and subsequent changes, are inaccurate, will also be found.

THE PUBLISHERS.

PUBLISHERS' PREFACE
TO THE FIFTH EDITION.

It affords us great pleasure to place before the photographic public the fifth edition of this work, which has proved to be one of the most valuable and popular publications that has ever been issued on any photographic subject.

THE PUBLISHERS.

THE FERROTYPE,

AND HOW TO MAKE IT.

CHAPTER I.

POSITIVE PHOTOGRAPHY.

Positive Photography embraces all that class of pictures made by the action of light through a camera lens on prepared sensitized surfaces, such as Daguerreotype, Ambrotype, and the Ferrotype.

The term is also used to designate that branch of Photography more generally denominated "printing," or the action of light through a negative on sensitized paper.

The sense in which we shall use it, will be to distinguish that class of pictures which are made directly in the camera, from the ordinary photograph. We call an Ambrotype a positive picture, to distinguish it from a negative, which is, after all, only an Ambrotype over-timed and over-developed; but that excess of development completely changes the character of the resulting image.

The chief characteristics of positive pictures are, ease and facility of production, beauty and delicacy of chemical effect and tone, and, (according to the surface on which made,) their complimentary tendency.

The Daguerreotype, to this day, is a marvel of beauty and delicacy, because of the fine and polished surface on which it is made, giving brilliant contrasts of light and shade, and an unapproachable delicacy and finish to the whole picture.

The Ambrotype would probably be equal to the Daguerreotype in all points but for the lack of brilliancy caused by the absorption of light by collodion film and the glass on which the picture is made.

While the Ferrotype, however, approaches nearer the Daguerreotype in all its points of excellence than any other picture of its kind, it is still inferior in brilliancy to the latter, for the reason that its surface is not finely polished, it is less opaque, the varnished collodion surface will not reflect light so perfectly as the polished silver; but while it is not equal to the Daguerreotype in that respect, it has compensatory advantages which have placed it far in advance of any other product in positive photography.

The same excellencies that were claimed for the beautiful productions of Daguerre, are now claimed for the Ferrotype in conjunction with other advantages, among which may be mentioned rapidity of production, greater portability, adaptation to far more extended use, and last but not least, cheapness—these qualities have made the Ferrotype the picture for the million, for while a Ferrotypist can produce pictures combining and exhibiting all the excellencies which distinguished the most artistic productions of photography, there will not lack the cultivated and refined to admire the picture and patronize the artist—and while a number of such pictures can be made and finished to the waiting customer, there will be many hurried business men, impatient travelers, anxious to catch a train, friends about to part, and others, to whom occasions and circumstances render a likeness obtainable, at once, desirable; keeping the gallery thronged, and amply rewarding the skillful operator.

While likenesses can be produced at a trifling cost, there will be thousands in the humbler walks of life desirous of gratifying that universal passion, the craving to possess some memento of the passing moment in this world of change. The desire to perpetuate the face and form upon which Time is day by day doing its marvelous and changeful work—so long, I say, as these feelings, desires, and circumstances exist and exert an influence on our lives, so long will the Ferrotype be a popular picture; and ever increasingly so, as population shall multiply, as time shall cause separation and changes, as families shall be broken up and scattered over this broad land, and in fine, while Death, the destroyer, shall remain in our midst, taking from us the dear ones we love, the noble ones we respect, and the great, who are the pride and admiration of the country.

Time, while working all these changes, shall increase our knowledge, add skill to the artist, and improve the artistic taste and judgment of the people—but it is very doubtful if time shall produce any other style of portraiture which shall supersede the Ferrotype, or reduce it to a lower place than its present high position in popular estimation.

The productions of Positive Photography are all of them famous? The Daguerreotype, as the first, had a brief but triumphant day. It made its advent as one of the wonders of the world, and excited as much admiration, perhaps, as did the telegraph, in the minds of the people; it was welcomed as a greater boon to the masses than was the telegraph, but unlike the telegraph, which remains to us at this day, substantially as the lamented Morse sent it, to do its work of annihilating time, the Daguerreotype has passed from popular favor, has been superseded by other methods of portraiture as far ahead of it as it was in advance of the productions of the itinerant miniature painters or silhouette cutters.

It is unnecessary that any account of the origin of the Daguerreotype process should be given in this connection, but it might furnish interesting matter for thought to readers; therefore we copy the following from an authentic English publication, which occupies on the shelves of our libraries, the place of greatest convenience and access.

Photography may be said to date its origin from the time of Baptista Porta, who invented the camera obscura in the 16th century. Between this period and the time of Wedgewood and Davy, only a few isolated facts bearing upon the subject were brought to light at intervals. It would profit but little to notice these in the order in which they occurred, but it is nevertheless interesting to observe in all great discoveries how small are the beginnings, as will be seen by the perusal of the following account of Wedgewood's discovery. The property possessed by the salts of silver, when decomposed by the action of light, was well known to the earlier chemists, and M. Charles, a well known French physician, exhibited in his lectures at the Louvre, a paper capable of taking silhouette figures by the action of solar light, but he has left no account of his process. Mr. Wedgewood, therefore, was undoubtedly the first person who recorded his attempts to use the sunbeams for Photographic printing. In the year 1802 he published a paper in the Journal of the Royal Institution, which he described as "an ac-"count of a method of copying paintings upon "glass, and making profiles by the agency of "light upon nitrate of silver; with observations "by H. Davy," a gentleman afterward better known as Sir Humphrey Davy. From this paper the earliest we are acquainted with, in which the discovery of these processes present themselves, the following extracts are taken: "White paper, or white leather moistened with a solution of nitrate of silver undergoes no change when kept in the dark; but on being exposed to the daylight, it speedily changes color, and after passing through different shades of gray and brown, becomes at length nearly black. The alteration of color takes place more speedily in proportion, as the light is more intense. In the direct beam of the sun, two or three minutes are sufficient to produce the full effect, in the shade, several hours are required, and a light transmitted through different colored glasses act with different degrees of intensity. Thus it is found that red rays have very little effect upon it; yellow and green are more effective, but violet or blue produce the most powerful effects.

"When the shadow of any figure is thrown upon the prepared surface, the part concealed by it remains white, and the other parts speedily become dark. For copying paintings on glass, the solution should be applied on leather, and in this case, it is more readily acted on than when paper is used. After color has been once fixed on the leather or paper, it can not be removed by the application of water, or water and soap, and it is in a high degree permanent. The copy of a painting or the profile immediately taken, must be placed in an obscure place; it may, indeed, be examined in the shade, but in this case, the exposure should be only for a few minutes; by the lights of candles or lamps, as commonly employed, it is not sensibly affected. No attempt that has been made to prevent the uncolored parts of the copy or profile being acted on by the light, have as yet been successful. They have been covered by a coating of fine varnish, but this has not destroyed their susceptibility of becoming colored, and even after repeated washings, sufficient of the active part will adhere to the white parts of the leather or paper to cause them to become dark when exposed to the rays of the sun. Besides the applications of this method of copying that has just been mentioned, there are many others, and it will be useful in making delineations of all such objects as are possessed of a texture, partly opaque and partly transparent. The woody fibers of leaves, and the wings of insects may be pretty accurately represented by means of it, and in this case it is only necessary to cause the direct solar light to pass through them, and to receive the shadows on leather.

"The image formed by means of a camera obscura have been found to be too faint to produce in any moderate time, an effect upon the nitrate of silver." To copy these images was the first object of Mr. Wedgewood in his researches on the subject, and for the purpose he first used nitrate of silver, which was mentioned to him by a friend as a substance very sensible to the influence of light, but all his numerous experiments as to their primary end proved unsuccessful. "In following these processes, I have found that the image of small objects, produced by means of the solar microscope, may be copied without difficulty on prepared paper. This will probably be a useful application of this method; that it may be employed successfully, however, it is necessary that the paper be placed at but a small distance from the lens."

Here we have the first indication of this great discovery. Subsequently, about the years 1810-11, Seebeck made some interesting discoveries as to the production of color on chloride of silver by solar radiations; the violet rays rendering it brown, the blue producing a shade of blue, the yellow preserving it white, and the red constantly giving a red shade to the salt.

BERARD'S DISCOVERY.—In the year 1812, M. Berard, brought the result of some valuable researches before a commission, composed of MM. Berthollet, Chaptal, and Biot, who state in their report that M. Berard had discovered that the chemical intensity was greatest at the violet end of the spectrum, and that it extended as Ritter, and Wollaston had previously observed, a little beyond that extremity where he left substances exposed for a certain time to the action of each ray: he observed sensible effects, though with an intensity continually decreasing in the indigo and blue rays. Hence, they considered it as extremely probable that if he had been able to employ agents still more sensible, he would have observed analogous effects. To show plainly the great disproportion which exists in this respect between the energies of different colored rays, M. Berard, concentrated by means of a lens, all that part of a spectrum which extends from the green to the extreme violet; he also concentrated by another lens all that portion which extended from the green to the extremity of the red; this last pencil formed a white so brilliant that the eyes were scarcely able to endure it, yet the nitrate of silver remained exposed more than two hours to this brilliant point of light without undergoing any sensible alteration. On the other hand, when exposed to the other rays, which were much less bright and less hot, it was blackened in less than six minutes. After some further remarks on the importance of M. Berard's experiments they proceed as follows: "If we consider solar light as composed of three distinct substances, one of which occasions *light*, the other *heat*, and the third *chemical combinations*, it will follow that each of these substances is separable by the prism into the infinity of different modifications like light itself; since we find by experiment that each of these properties is spread, though unequally, over a certain extent of the spectrum, and we must suppose on that hypothesis, that there exists *three* spectrums, one above the other; namely, a Calorific, a Colorific, and a Chemical Spectrum. We must likewise admit that each of the substances which compose the three spectrums, and even each molecule of unequal refrangibility which constituted these substances is endowed, like the molecules of visible light, with the property of being polarized by reflection, and of escaping from reflection in the same positions as the luminous molecules."

From that time numerous experiments were conducted by several eminent researchers, including the discoveries of the more celebrated MM. Niepce and Daguerre.

DAGUERRE AND NIEPCE'S DISCOVERY.—To the inventive genius of these gentlemen we are indebted for the first application of this great discovery, but, like most great conceptions of the human mind, this art, as we have seen, advanced by slow steps, and was indicated from time to time by the isolated facts we have briefly alluded to.

The researches of M. Niepce were commenced in 1814, but it was not till 1826 that he was made aware by the indiscretion of an optician employed by both, that M. Daguerre was pursuing the same course of experiments. A correspondence between the two philosophers was the result, and henceforth their researches were pursued in common, and, some years later, resulted in the discovery of this branch of the art, since known as the Daguerreotype.

In 1833 M. Niepce died, having communicated all his discoveries to M. Daguerre, and in 1839 that gentleman, with a most laudible abnegation of self, communicated his discoveries to the public.

As is well known, the Daguerreotype picture receives its name from one of its discoverers; it is taken on a copper plate with a silvered surface. We have seen that the paper process and afterward the glass-plates, coated with various organic substances, have greatly superseded the silvered plate, especially in this country; but as a branch of photographic art it forms an interesting chapter.

The beautiful process by which the Daguerreotype picture is obtained was published to the world in July, 1839, after the French Government of the day had rewarded M. Daguerre with a pension of 6,000 francs, and M. Isidore Niepce, the son of Daguerre's colleague in the discovery, with another of 4,000 francs, with a reversion of one-half to their widows; a liberal endowment, worthy of imitation on the part of any enlightened government.

Then follows a very lengthy and minutely particular account of the process for making Daguerreotypes, which would prove of no interest to the readers of this work.

Of the Ambrotype, it is not necessary to say more than that it, like the Ferrotype, is made by the collodion process—the first on glass, the latter on Japanned iron—the history of the invention and manufacture of which is given elsewhere as being in harmony with the purposes of this book.

As it is the intention of the writer that the beginner shall find in these pages every thing that may be useful for him to know, in order that he may produce good work, we shall proceed to a careful description of the processes and manipulations pertaining to the Ferrotype in the next chapter.

CHAPTER II.

THE FERROTYPE.

From the time of the introduction of the collodion process and photography on glass by Messrs. Archer and Horne of England, no one invention or discovery has given a greater impetus to the art, than the introduction of the Melanotype or Ferrotype plate in the years 1856–57.

The Ambrotype, which at that time held the field, was not calculated for a very extended usefulness, from the heavy, brittle nature of the substance (glass) on which it was made. In fact, Ambrotypes were only suitable for cases and small frames, not at all for many of the purposes that make the chief demand of the Ferrotype.

The brittle character of glass, also unfitted it

as a vehicle for a picture, which, however little it may have cost originally, there are so many contingencies under which its value to the owner might become incalculable, not in money or other earthly dross, but as the last memento of one, in whose existence might have centered the hopes and aspirations of many tender hearts, and upon whom may have been lavished the holiest and tenderest feelings of our nature.

Again, glass, besides being brittle in its nature, is heavy and bulky, and, in consequence, was not suitable for other than small miniatures, such as were destined to be put in small cases or frames, to be carried on the person or to lie on the parlor table or mantel-piece. How many a happy home there is, upon whose table may be found these tokens of friendship or love, and how much better would it be if those Ambrotypes could be transformed into the imperishable Ferrotype, and placed in the elegant parlor picture album, thus placing them almost above the power of accident or the possibility of loss.

Many of the readers of these pages, who, like the writer, made Ambrotypes on white and afterward on colored glass, will recollect how rapidly the glass plate gave way before the advancing popularity of the Ferrotype, which, in a short time, entirely superseded its older rival, and at this present time bids fair to excel every other branch of the art in the amount and magnitude of the interests involved in its production.

The Ferrotype, when first introduced, merely took the place of the Ambrotype and other positive pictures; that is, they were made and fitted in cases and frames, etc., in precisely the same manner as the Ambrotype, Daguerreotype, etc., had been before, but for the Ferrotype there were possibilities of usefulness and application that were not open to its less fortunate predecessors.

There soon began to be a demand for them for other purposes than to enclose in cases, frames, etc. The lightness of the plate and the ability of the finished pictures to resist the effects of light, of dampness, and of friction, without any protection to the surface other than varnish, fitted them to be carried on the person without cases, and made it possible to send them to friends at a distance through the Post-office, for which purpose many were made and called "Letter-types." They also became very popular as miniatures for lockets, pins, rings, etc., for which purposes the extreme thinness of the plate made them peculiarly well adapted, while the brilliancy and beauty of the picture gives them the first place in adaptation to such purposes.

In the shape and size of the "cartes de visite" or album picture, they also soon became immensely popular—in this size and also that of the larger card, the "Imperial," the most beautiful and brilliant effects are capable of being produced; so much so, that when on the occasion of the meeting of the "National Photographer's Convention," in Philadelphia, in 1871, the writer exhibited in a very quiet manner an album full of his productions in these two sizes they excited the utmost admiration, and increased immensely the respect of some of the members for the Ferrotype.

But it was in the shape of the "Gem" Ferrotype that the greatest number of these pictures have been sold. These "Gems" are made by the multiplying camera with four or more lenses, and two or more consecutive exposures, and they differ in size from that of sixteen on a quarter plate to four on the same. They are made very quickly and sold very cheaply, ranging from ten cents the dozen, unmounted, to fifty cents with paper mounts.

The writer has made of these, with his own hands, as many as one hundred and twenty dozen in one day, and sold every dozen at fifty cents, never having before or since sold a dozen for less.

These pictures have a peculiar interest to the children, and in the cities it is impossible to compute the number or quantities which have been made and sold since 1860. I suppose it would exceed that of all other pictures put together.

As a branch of Photography, the production of Ferrotypes has now attained to such magnitude that large establishments are fitted up and exclusively devoted to the production of this popular picture—for the information of those about to open galleries for Ferrotypes or any other branch of Photography, we propose to describe such an establishment, and to give an account of the collodion process as applied to Ferrotypes.

CHAPTER III.

THE FERROTYPE GALLERY

Requires a Reception Room or salesroom fitted up for the reception of customers and for the sale of the productions of the gallery, as also cases, frames, and such other articles as are usually sold in establishments of this kind. There should be a counter show-case in which to expose such articles, with sample pictures, etc., a desk for the books of the establishment, chairs, tables, etc.; leading from this should be a dressing-room for ladies and another for gentlemen, each appropriately furnished with conveniences of the toilet, such as basins for water, mirrors, combs, brushes, etc., minute details of which are unnecessary. In the reception room some means should be provided for the entertainment of customers where delays occur, or when kept waiting by others occupying the attention of the artist—an effort to keep people in good humor while waiting, always produces good results and pays in the greater facility of pleasing them when their pictures are made. For this purpose, the walls should be tastefully decorated with the samples of the best productions of the gallery. As an example, some of the most beautiful and artistic work in this country may be seen on the walls of well-known galleries in this and other cities. The reception room of the gallery may be rendered pleasant, delightfully so, by this and other means, such as a centre-table provided with books, papers, and magazines, a musical instrument, a stereoscope, or as in some a few pots of choice flowers, a small fountain with fish, an aquarium, or a few song birds. Various means are adapted to this purpose according to the taste and culture of the proprietor, or to suit the character and means of the people it is expected to entertain and please.

An album filled with choicest examples of all the different sizes of Ferrotypes may be kept on the show-case, to be examined by customers for sizes, style, and price. But, above all, an attentive and obliging attendant should be in the reception room to receive orders and wait upon, talk to, and keep in good temper, the many impatient ones waiting their turn in the posing chair.

A capable person, male or female, can earn their own salary over and above the regular work of the gallery by careful attention to customers and a suggestion now and then.

The Glass or Operating Room comes next, and should be furnished with

Backgrounds,	Reflectors,
Camera Stands,	Camera Boxes,
Lenses,	Focussing Glasses,
Posing Chairs,	Head Rests,
Copying Stand,	Head Cloths,
Curtain,	Curtain Stand,
Table,	Table Cover,
Ottomans,	

Finishing Table, provided with gas or naphtha stove or dryer, varnish, colors, color brushes, color blender, etc., etc.

CHAPTER IV.

THE GLASS ROOM.

There is no subject which so greatly concerns the Ferrotypist as the construction of the Glass Room, or operating room, as it is more generally denominated in this country. The construction and arrangement of the Glass Room depends altogether upon the judgment and experience of the Ferrotypist, and in most cases he is compelled to decide as to the proper shape and exposure of its lights or windows without outside help or advice; and may not, as in the case of apparatus, chemicals, etc., purchase ready-prepared of manufacturers of established reputation.

Those operators who may have traveled over the country, practicing their art in small country towns and at cross-roads, sometimes became very ingenious in the management of the lights of an ordinary window in a country tavern, or of the no less difficult light of a canvass tent or traveling saloon or car. This class of operator is never at a loss for some method of overcoming difficulties—they are fertile in expedients, they understand very well the uses of paper muslin and other fabrics suitable for the reflection of light. There are many, however, who have never been compelled to learn these things from so expensive a teacher as experience, and therefore have never learned how much depends upon the light in the production of good pictures, and in facilitating the operations of the gallery.

A few words of instruction and advice will, therefore, not be amiss in this connection.

In the construction of a Glass Room, then, there are a few things to be taken into consideration, viz., an abundance of light, in order that exposure may be short. A steady light least affected by shadows and clouds. A diffused light excluding direct rays. A light sufficiently elevated to soften the shadows and to give a more even illumination. A perpendicular fall of light to give brilliancy to the eye, definition to the drapery, etc., etc. A horizontal light to give strength and solidity, and to soften the shadows under the chin, nose, eyebrows, etc.

A light which will permit the operator to obtain from each face its best view and also its most characteristic expression.

A light which can be modified to suit the varying requirements of different faces, and can be made a perpendicular, horizontal, or oblique light at will; in short, a light which will facilitate a regular and continued success on the part of the operator.

There are, distinctively, but two kinds of lights, viz., the perpendicular or top light which comes from above, and the horizontal or side light, that which comes from an opening or window in the side of a perpendicular wall.

Neither of these two lights, separately, would meet the requirements above mentioned; but when built together, the lower end of the top resting upon the side light, they compose that particular form of light which the best photographers all over the country, and the world, perhaps, have generally agreed upon as the best; and only in this shape, with a northern exposure, can the varied requirements already specified be fully met.

There are many instances, however, of the impossibility of securing the advantages of the

"Combined" light. In many "out-of-the-way" places, where the presence of the peripatetic photographer is a blessing, must he deny himself the profit he hopes to derive, and the happiness he expects to confer, by the exercise of his art, because he can not have the advantages of the best style of light? I say, no! rather let him adapt himself to the circumstances, and make the *best* use of the facilities procurable, than to disappoint a community, some of whom, the meanest effort of his art might render inexpressibly happy.

It is certain that the clever operator will sometimes make good pictures under the most unfavorable circumstances; in many cases difficulties only stimulate to ingenuity in overcoming them, and in no instance known to the writer is there a greater demand for those qualities of invention and ingenuity, which enables their possessor to rise superior to every difficulty, than in the practice of photography, in any of its branches, under a small top light or beside a window in some lonely, out-of-the-way place, where the people are all sunburnt and rough-skinned, and even the pretty girls are sadly tanned by exposure to the weather.

The effect of a light falling from above, upon the features of a sitter directly under it, would be to exaggerate the projections of the brows, cheek bones, and nose, rendering the eyes cavernous or deep set, and throwing heavy shadows under the nose and chin; in many cases, the shadow under the chin assuming the shape of a beard, and that under the nose might look like a mustache if it were broader and more conformed to the shape of the lip. Very few operators would, however, think of posing a subject directly under a top light—he would shade the light, if it was plain glass, with a white muslin curtain, out of which all starch had been taken, and would be allowed to hang loosely in the middle, "bagging down," as it is called; this would give a diffused white light; the subject to be lighted would be seated under the ceiling, very near the opening through which the light falls from above. Reflectors of paper muslin or glazed cotton, as it is sometimes called, might be used to throw a reflected light wherever required, and in case the shadows under the eyebrows and nose were still too heavy and the cheeks appeared too hollow, a screen made of heavy paper stretched on a hoop or square frame, might be held over the head to intercept a portion of the light from above, care being taken not to spoil the catch-light, or small point of light in the eye, which gives brilliancy to that organ. By means of such appliances skillfully used, very good work may be produced, and great variety of effect obtained. Indeed, the authorities to the contrary notwithstanding, much better pictorial effects may be obtained from a top light skillfully managed than from a side light, however capable the operator may be—and yet much may be done to remedy the defects of such a light by the use of reflectors within the room and outside the window. Upon seating a person beside a window with one side exposed, the effect produced is called the "hatchet" expression, the face assuming a wedge-like appearance, one side being illuminated and the other in the shade; the illuminated side is flattened by the strong light, and the opposite side by the heavy shadow. Now, it would be as ridiculous for me to instance such an effect as the best that could be procured by a side light, as to instance the deep-set eyes, the hollow cheeks, and dense shadows under the projections of the face, as the best that could be produced by a top light. These effects are examples, merely, of the primary and unmodified effects of these distinctive lights. In the case of the light under consideration, much may be done to change the character of the "hatchet" expression, and to remove the unpleasant cat-like slit of light in the eye characteristic of the side light. Outside the window a reflector may be placed at such an angle as to throw the light in an inward and upward direction, where it may be met by another reflector, which might be placed so as to throw the light downward upon the sitter, and with a reflector on the side opposite the light, the character of the illumination might be very materially improved. By seating a person opposite and fronting a side light or window, an illumination called a "front" light may be obtained, by some treated as a distinct variety of light, but which appears to me to be only another application of the side light. In combination with the top light, the front light might be very useful in some cases, but as a distinct style of lighting I can not conceive how it could ever be tolerated, as its effects take away all character and likeness from the face, filling the eyes with light, illuminating every line and depression equally with the projections, and giving a flat and meaningless expression to all faces alike.

There may be circumstances under which the Ferrotypist, in erecting for himself a glass room, will find it impossible to secure the combination of top and side light, and where the top, or indeed only a side light may be available. In

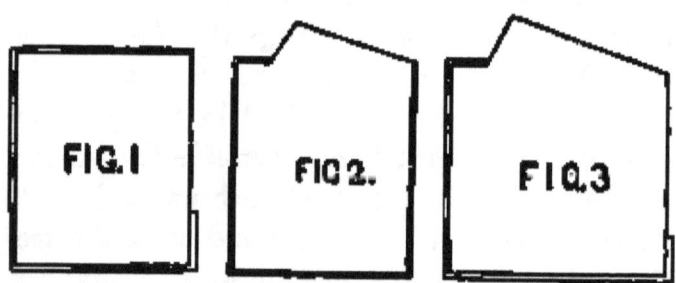

such cases, modified forms of top or side light, giving a much more favorable illumination, might be adopted.

We give in diagrams 1, 2, and 3, views of the side light, the top light, and of the combined top and side light; the double lines representing the walls, the single indicating the glazed parts.

Fig. 1 represents by the single line on the right side of the diagram, the side light, or that form of light which can be used as a side or front light, a few hints for working which, have already been given.

Fig. 2 shows the general shape of a top light; the pitch may be made greater or less. It is perhaps better that the top light be made with considerable pitch, as by this means it more perfectly sheds the rainwater and we obtain a more oblique light. In small towns, and in the country, where the roofs of houses are not flat but like the letter A, a light 10 or 12 feet square let into the roof makes a very convenient and satisfactory light.

Where top lights are erected, the top of the room should be cut away so as leave a bevel or slope, from the sash of the window, widening as it descends, to the ceiling of the room, so as to allow the light to spread out, particularly on that side where the backgrounds are placed, to permit of an equal illumination of the ground from the bottom to the top.

Fig. 3 gives a view of the top and side combination, than which no form of light is better, and none other should be adopted where circumstances will permit. It is of equal importance that the side window should face the north.

The size or dimensions of the lights are

matters of no great importance beyond a certain point; that is, the top light should not be less than twelve feet square, the side being of the same width, extending from the top to within a foot of the floor. In some galleries the lights are exceedingly large, such as a length of 40 feet with a breadth of 20 feet from the top, and an equal length for the side—such an immense area of glass is superfluous, as indeed may be proved by work made in glass rooms of moderate size. There is no better work produced than in the galleries of New York, in no one of which is there a light of greater dimensions than 16 feet, and some of the best have even less. The light used by Mr. Kurtz, of New York, is the combined top and side with northern exposure, the top being placed at an angle of 45°, is 10 feet square, on which joins the side light, 10 feet by 8 feet extending to the floor.

While the northern exposure is by far the best for photographic purposes, it does not, nor can it be constructed so as to exclude the sunlight; various devices have been resorted to by different operators to obviate this difficulty, among which board screens, awnings worked by pulleys from the inside, and, lately, a form of blind similar to the common outside window blinds with movable slats has been adopted, and found to be a success—the slats are light frames of wood, working on center pivots, and covered with muslin, canvas, or, indeed, made entirely of wood. (A good description of such an apparatus may be found in the "Philadelphia Photographer," for August, 1871, page 269.) By the use of these blinds, sunlight can be entirely excluded by setting them as we do the blinds outside the windows of our residences, so as to intercept the sunlight and not to exclude diffused light and air; they also serve the purpose of shading the glass from the extreme heat of the summer sun.

Heretofore, one great difficulty with top lights has been the leakage; indeed, it seemed to be almost impossible to secure a perfectly watertight Glass Room, until some ingenious person in Philadelphia invented the sash, named after the city where invented, of which the following diagram shows an end view. The letter A shows

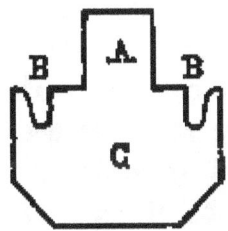

the ridge between the glass in which the fastenings which hold the glass are driven; on each side are the rests or supports for the glass, outside of which are grooves B, B, to receive the water that may leak through. In connection with this form of sash, the ends of the glass should be cut thus, the points extending upward, and lapped one over the other not more than one quarter of an inch; by cutting the glass in this manner, the water is caused to flow toward the

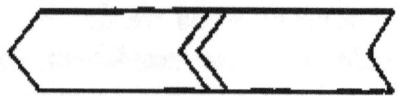

sides of the glass, where if any passes through, it falls into the grooves on each side of the sash, and is carried outside and falls into the leader or waste-pipe.

The best method of shading a light internally, is by narrow frames of wood or iron covered with paper or blue paper muslin, the frames or shades to be each about one foot wide, and fastened on pivots at each end so as to be easily turned, somewhat after the manner of the slats of a window-blind, one to overlap the other slightly when closed. These shades are in use in most first-class galleries. The next best plan is to have spring roller shades of blue or white muslin, controlled by cords and pulleys.

There should be at least two back-grounds: one white, the other scenic-exterior or interior, and made as light in color or tone as compatible with proper delineation. In cities, a rustic fence with proper scenic grounds gives great satisfaction, both for groups and single figures; and reasoning from that, I should suppose that a handsome interior, with suitable accessories, would give more satisfaction in country places.

There should be a reflector for each light; the reflector should be covered on one side with white, and on the other with blue paper muslin, the glazed side out, and hung on pivots in a light frame with casters, so that it may be easily moved. It is to be used on the side opposite the light, to relieve heavy shadows under projecting parts of the face, and the shaded side of the object or sitter.

One camera stand will generally be found sufficient, but if business is brisk, with the necessity of changing boxes, two will be found very useful. There are a great many different kinds of stands in use, and the purchaser will rarely have any difficulty in choosing the best. It will be well to secure one that will combine lightness and durability.

Of camera boxes, owing to their importance to the Ferrotyper, it will be proper to enter more into detail; especially of the kind which, from the facility by which large numbers of pictures are produced by their use, are called

MULTIPLYING CAMERAS.

Before the invention of the Multiplier, Ferrotypes were made singly of the regular photographic sizes, and sold in cases or frames. As the introduction of the cartes-de-visite in photography created a wonderful change and growth in the business, so did the invention of the Multiplying box, whereby from one to 50 or 100 pictures could be made on one plate at the same time, by consecutive exposures through one or more lenses, increase and extend the popularity of the Ferrotype. Any means whereby a dozen pictures could be made in about the space of time previously required to make one by the old method, would enable the operator to sell a dozen at or near the same price as he formerly demanded for one—and then, a dozen "Gem" Ferrotypes could be made and mounted on cards, or set in preservers, or merely cut apart, and be sold for 50 cents, while very few artists ever thought of charging less than that sum for one, set in a case.

At the present time, no gallery can be considered to be furnished without a Multiplying Camera box, for they are as useful in all other branches of photography as they are in making Ferrotypes.

It is claimed that the first Multiplier was made, and a patent procured for the same, by Mr. Albert Southworth, of Boston, Mass., and however successfully that claim may be disputed, it is not denied that the first boxes of the kind were made and sold as Multiplying boxes by Mr. Simon Wing, originally of Waterville, Maine, under Mr. Southworth's patent, of which Mr. Wing became the purchaser, in conjunction with Mr. Marcus Ormsbee, of Boston.

For some ten or twelve years past, Mr. Wing has manufactured these boxes in Boston, Mass., and has sold them only to those who were able and willing to buy the patent right for the town or county in which they wished to use the same.

By such an illiberal and exclusive policy, he has rendered it profitable for others engaged in the manufacture of camera boxes to make and sell innumerable infringements on Southworth's patent, and thus entailed on himself numerous law suits to maintain the validity and the rights guaranteed by the patent.

It is conceded by the general public, and established by law, that the man who invents a new and useful piece of apparatus, a new and useful machine, a labor-saving instrument or engine, or who discovers a new process or novel application of power or force, or a new combination of any kind, if he can establish and make good his claim before the officers appointed by law to inquire into such matters; shall be protected in the exclusive use, manufacture, or sale of such invention or discovery, as far as the law can so protect, for it can not be denied that beyond a certain point the law is of no avail to protect a man in such exclusive use or sale; indeed, the law is unable to protect the government itself against the aggressions of those to whom the law makes such aggression profitable. Let the tax on any one article of importation be made so high as to render smuggling profitable, and behold with what difficulty smuggling is put down; let the tax on whisky be put at $2.00 a gallon and we see the whole force of the government paralyzed, and whisky sold in defiance of law at less than the tax. So, too, with any patented article of great usefulness, let the price be fixed so high by the patentee as to render infringement profitable, notwithstanding the risk; and infringements will be made. So it was with Wing's Multiplying Camera box, manufactured of the best materials expressly selected for the purpose, under the eye of a practical photographer and mechanic, serviceable and durable; the price was fixed so high, and even more than that, the necessity of procuring a town or county right with the box, rendered the manufacture of infringements so profitable, that thousands were made and sold with impunity all over the country. As a natural consequence, lawsuits followed; in one of which, Wing, of Boston, against C. C. Schoonmaker, of Troy, New York, after having been carried to the Supreme Court of the United States, the patent received its quietus by a tie vote of eight judges, the Chief-Justice being absent.

It is to be hoped that the above may be a warning to inventors who may be inclined to ask too much for their valuable inventions, as is in general the case, especially with photographers.

Multiplying Cameras may now be had of a great variety of patterns, most of which are as serviceable and useful in small galleries as the best made. The varieties most used, however are those made by Wing of Boston, by the American Optical Company, of New York, and the Success Camera boxes, sold by E. & H. T. Anthony, also of New York. In principle these boxes are the same, only differing in design or pattern and in the indicators, and arrangements for making the various movements. They are of all sizes and suited to all varieties of work.

The half plate box, so called, (few are made of a smaller size), will make with a single tube, one, two, four, six or sixteen pictures on a quarter plate by as many moves; with four tubes it will make, on a quarter plate, four pictures by one exposure, eight by two exposures, or sixteen "gems" by four exposures. On a half plate eight pictures by two exposures, thirty-two by eight exposures—with four tubes. The 5 by 7 Victoria box, with one tube, will make two Victoria portraits by two exposures. One imperial or cabinet size by one exposure, four cartes-de-visite by four moves, and with four tubes, sixteen gems on a quarter plate and thirty-two on a half plate—with nine tubes, nine, eighteen or thirty-six on 5 by 7 plate, according to size. The 4-4 or whole plate box is probably most useful, as it embraces the whole range of sizes, both in plates from 1-9 to 4-4, and in pictures from one on 4-4, any size, to sixty-four on 4-4 plate. There are other boxes made but they are useful only where vast quantities of pictures are made at exceedingly low prices, as if you were to make them by the bushel. These boxes are, or should be, accompanied by printed directions for making the various movements for the different sizes of pictures, or for selecting and placing the openings or diaphrams, which are set in the back of the box immediately in front of the ground glass, through which the picture is made.

It requires some few days to become familiar with the management of a good multiplier, those made by Wing requiring rather longer to learn than others; but when once learned, they are easy to remember and practice, and are very accurate in operation.

The multiplier is chiefly valuable to the ferrotyper to enable him to make pictures in numbers. Many prefer the ferrotype to the photograph, and would pay as much for a dozen good ferrotypes as for a dozen cartes-de-visite; and by the use of this box the operator can make and deliver to a waiting customer a dozen pictures, which will afford more satisfaction probably than twelve cartes-de-visite made at the same price.

We have undertaken no history of the multiplier in this connection, but only wish to inform the fraternity that there are a variety of sizes and patterns of these boxes, and to illustrate the fable, the moral of which is, "*Be sure not to grasp too much, or you will lose all.*"

The multiplier may be used with one lens or with four, six or nine. Generally the sizes less than the 4-4 are not fitted to use more than four of the small or Gem tubes, and one-quarter, half, extra half or a quick acting lens of the two-thirds size. The larger boxes are fitted with blocks of nine of the small tubes, four of the quarter size, or one of the 4-4 or larger sizes; therefore the 4-4 box has a greater range of usefulness, for by their use one, four, eight or sixteen pictures can be made on a quarter plate, and on the larger ones a proportionate number, according to the size of the plate. These cameras are generally provided with two plate-holders, to the proper care of which attention should be given. The frames for the reception of various sizes of plates are not provided with glass or composition corners, but are made with a rabbet all round, in order that every side of the plate may rest firmly. A piece of glass of the same size as the plate, is placed at the back of the plate and forced closely forward by the action of a spring on the door at the back of the holder. When new these frames and the holder should be placed in boiling oil and completely saturated, so that the silver solution may not soak into the wood when in active use. Another good plan is to take parafine and apply it in a melted state to the frames and holder; its effects is to repel the silver and prevent its action on the wood. The holders, when in constant use, should also be varnished about once a week with a solution of gum shellac dissolved in wood naphtha, which is an excellent varnish, impervious to the silver solution, at the same time preventing any chemical action on the plate from contact with the wood.

LENSES.—There are a great many lenses in the market, among which it is difficult to choose. My experience proves that of the smaller Gem tubes, those of Darlot á Paris are the best; of the other sizes there is no great difference among the cheap instruments, and if it is desired to procure a larger tube of the 4-4 size, or even larger, then it is advisable to procure of the more expensive manufacture, always keeping in mind that whatever lenses you may purchase, be sure to make rapidity of action one of the qualities most to be desired. A 4-4 multiplier, provided with nine "Gem" tubes, four quarter and one 4-4 or extra do, should be enough for most galleries where the business is confined to the production of Ferrotypes.

FOCUSSING GLASS.—The focussing glass is a very useful article, and every camera box should be provided with one. Their use is to magnify the image on the object glass so as more easily to secure a perfect focus.

POSING CHAIRS.—Posing chairs are now in general use and are in great variety. In selecting, choose one of the most graceful design and best finish. A great revolution in the style and finish of these useful chairs was made, I think, in 1866, by the introduction at that date of "Sarony's Universal Rest and Posing Chair." Mr. Sarony sold immense numbers of them, until they indeed became universal in use. The most popular poising chairs are now made in imitation of the shape of the Sarony chair, with which most photographers are already familiar.

HEAD RESTS.—Head rests are also in great variety of shapes, sizes and weight. The purchaser can very soon make up his mind as to his choice, after attempting to drag a sample of each kind across the room. The rest is, and should be so considered, indispensable in every gallery, so much so, that sittings should never be made without the use of the rest, except in the case of children. Much attention is now being given to the invention or discovery of means whereby the exposure of plates may be very materially shortened, for it is only by the use of extremely sensitive preparations or very quick acting lenses that we may be enabled to dispense with the head rest.

CURTAIN SUPPORT.—A head rest with a long iron rod, the top of which is bent at a right-angle, is about as useful for the support of a curtain as any other. The curtain, when of fine material and properly used, gives much pictorial effect to the Ferrotype. The use of the curtain is considered of so much importance that the National Photographic Society, at their convention in St. Louis this year, gave one of the medals designed for the most useful inventions introduced within this year, to Mr. Biglow, for his imitation silk curtain and graduating revolving back-ground.

COPYING STAND.—The copying stand is an important and necessary article of furniture in the operating room. They are sold by most photographic stock and apparatus dealers in various forms and designs, some of which are patented, and others not. A copying stand, which is cheap and as good as the best, is a narrow table strongly made of pine, not over eighteen inches wide and about four feet long. At one end an upright piece of board about eighteen inches square should be fastened perpendicularly, at a perfect right-angle with the table. Against one side of the table a strip of board should be firmly fixed, to form a guide to keep the camera in position, when focused upon a picture about to be copied. The picture to be copied is of course secured against the upright piece of wood by two or more tacks or sharp points kept for the purpose. With such a stand much greater certainty is attained, in securing more perfect copies. One or more drawers may be fitted underneath the table, to hold such centre stops and other articles as may be necessary and useful for this part of the business. I can not better illustrate the use and value of such a stand, than by referring the reader to an article on copying, on page 53 of "Photographic Mosaics" for 1871.

TABLE COVER.—The table and cover can be used with great advantage in many pictures, and is quite indispensable in a well appointed gallery. In selecting a table good taste, should be exhibited in the choice. A handsome black walnut table with ornamented top produces a very nice effect. A small table with white marble top is also conspicuously agreeable in pictorial effect. The table is often necessary to support articles required to be exhibited by the sitter or sitters, and will be frequently used to support articles required to be photographed alone. The table cover may very frequently—if of suitable material and color—be used as drapery falling over the back of a chair or resting carelessly on the floor to hide the foot of the head rest. There are many ways in which its usefulness may be exemplified.

OTTOMANS.—Ottomans, or hassocks, are very useful as low seats in the composition of groups, and should be liberally provided in every glass room. They can be made very useful in making with them, fanciful seats for children, the table cover or other drapery being thrown over the ottoman.

In galleries where there is not ample space for a furnishing room, a corner of the operating room is generally set apart for that purpose—this corner should be provided with a table about breast high, with a large and small drawer. Upon the table should be placed a gas or naphtha stove; if in a city where gas is procurable, naphtha should not be used, but when gas is not to be had, naphtha is the least objectionable substitute. Upon the stove should rest a wedge-shaped heater, against which the plates may be placed to dry, and again after being varnished. The plate when dry is to be colored or tinted. In the small drawer of the table should be kept a color box and brushes; the color best adapted for the face is Indian Red, with a small portion of silver white carefully and thoroughly mixed with it. The cheeks and lips of the picture may now be carefully colored, the superfluous color being brushed off with a small camel's hair blender, which also serves to soften the outlines of the color, and blends it off gradually to the white of the picture. The picture may now be varnished and set up against the stove to dry, a gentle heat being necessary to impart a gloss to the varnished surface, as it becomes dry and hard. A great many varnishes are advertised and sold as peculiarly suitable to Ferrotypes, and many of the varieties are good and perhaps better than the Ferrotypist could make for himself. Here the question of economy comes in, and should counterbalance any inferiority there may be in the domestic manufacture. Where very little varnish is used, however, it is better perhaps to order from your stock dealer, and so also with collodion and other mixtures. A very good quality of varnish may be made from shellac dissolved in alcohol. The alcohol should be the best and strongest obtainable; secure a wide mouth bottle, which will hold one gallon. Get the best quality of bleached shellac, break it up fine and small, put one pound in the bottle and fill up with alcohol. Set the bottle away for a few days, giving it a good shaking once in awhile; after the gum has dissolved and settled, decant the clear portion, after testing, to learn if it is thick enough; if not shake up and allow to stand—if too thick, dilute with alcohol and use. By keeping the stock bottle full, adding new shellac as required, you have, with very little trouble, a fine quality of varnish, giving with a gentle heat as fine a gloss to your work as any it is possible to make. Now, that the picture is dry, cut apart; if more than one, trim the edges, mount or place in envelopes, and they are ready to deliver.

CHAPTER V.

THE DARK ROOM.

The "dark room," as it is generally denominated, should not be in reality a dark room, it being only necessary to exclude the actinic rays of light. Light, then, may be admitted to any extent through colored glass, if that color is non-actinic. The best glass for this purpose is orange or yellow; the whole room may be made of glass of this color, and the work proceed without injury to the most sensitive film. Care must always be taken to *exclude all white light*—no cracks should be left open, doors should fit closely, and every other ingress for light carefully guarded. That the dark room should be the neatest and cleanest room in the building is the usual theory, but it is only necessary that it should be clean, free from dust, entirely so, and with as few shelves as possible.

A small dark room is best for the Ferrotype business, where every thing can be reached with little motion, with space to turn conveniently. This room should be furnished with a convenient supply of water under immediate control. A large trough-sink occupying the middle of one side; on each hand shelves—that on the right for the bath, the plate-holders and the developing solutions; those on the left for the collodion bottles and the plates. For a Ferrotype Gallery where pictures are made in sizes, from one on a quarter plate, to as large as 8 by 10 inches, the furniture and supplies of the dark room should be

   Ferro-plates,
   Collodion,
         Alcohol,
         Ether,
         Iodide of Ammonium,
         Iodide Cadmium,
         Bromide Cadmium,
         Gun Cotton.

   2. Collodion Bottles,
    Silver Solution:

         Nitrate of Silver,
         Iodide of Potassium,
         18 by 10 glass bath dish,
          with box and dipper.

Developing Solution:
>Protosulphate of Iron,
>Acetic Acid,
>Alcohol.

2 Decanting or Pouring Bottles,
1 Graduate, 8 or 16 oz.,
1 One-gallon funnel,
2 Small funnels,
8 by 10 glass dish, with box and dipper.

Fixing Solution:
>Cyanide of Potassium,

1 Evaporating dish,
1 Actino Hydrometer, single degree,
1 Package of filtering paper,
1 Package of filtering cotton,
1 Rack to hold wet plates,
Cotton flannel for cleaning plates.

The following diagram represents a dark room and the location of the sink, etc.

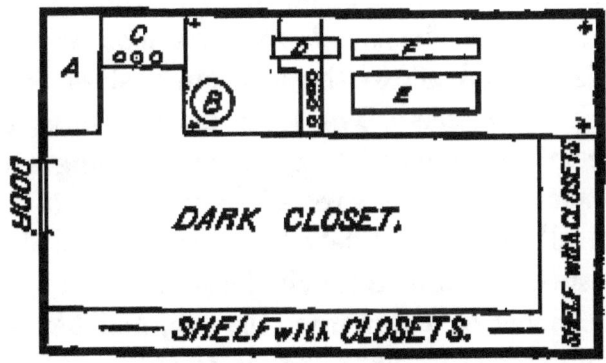

In this diagram the * * * * show the position and size of the sink, which is a strong wooden tank made perfectly water-tight and resting on the floor; the top is partly covered. On the left, at A, is a shelf for plates; C represents the position of the collodion bottles, F the bath dish, the top of which projects through the cover of the sink, the box resting on a shelf below in the tank. At E the holders rest on an inclined shelf, something like the top of a desk. The plate, having been coated with collodion, is placed in the bath at F; taken thence when coated, and placed in the holder at E, from whence it is taken to be exposed. After exposure it is removed from the holder and developed over the funnel B by the solution in bottles at G. After development it is washed under a faucet, which is over and between B, the funnel, and G, the developer shelf; it is then dipped in the cyanide bath at D (this bath should always be kept covered except when in use); the plate is again washed carefully and taken out to finish. Across the side opposite the tank, and across the end, are shelves under which are closets. The tank extends from the floor to a convenient height for developing over, and should be so constructed, in order that it may hold all the water likely to be used in one day; a waste-pipe passes through the side or end about nine inches or a foot from the top, and bending down extends in that direction to within three or four inches of the bottom. In this pipe outside the tank, should be a stop-cock; the hole where it passes through into the tank should be made water-tight. After a day's work, if the tank is full, a small quantity of a saturated solution of copperas (the commonest salt of iron) should be thrown into the tank, for the purpose of precipitating the silver that may be in the water. It should be left all night, to allow time for the precipitate to fall to the bottom. In the morning the stop-cock should be turned and the water allowed to run off, which it will do readily, the waste-pipe acting as a syphon. It will be necessary, however, that the tank should be full of water, or at least that the water should be above the top of the waste-pipe, in order that it may run out, for the water must be high enough to flow through the pipe when the stop-cock is turned, after which it will continue to run until all is exhausted. A tank arranged as thus described is the best silver-saving apparatus that can be devised. It receives all the washings of the plates, all the waste of the developing and fixing solutions, all the silver solution that may be wasted from the bath dish in raising the dipper many times a day, all the drippings of plates, all the films which should be rubbed from rejected plates or off the edges of all plates after development. These are all readily precipitated by the solution of iron, which costs but a trifle by the quantity. The precipitate, which is a thick black mud, may be taken from the tank once a year, or oftener if the business is large, and given to competent men for the reduction and separation of the silver it may contain.

CHAPTER VI.

COLLODION.

Collodion, according to Webster, is "a solution of gun-cotton in ether. It is strongly adhesive, and is used by surgeons to close up wounds. It is also employed in Photography."

Mr. Archer who, in conjunction with Mr. Horne, was the first to introduce this important addition to the art, deserves our utmost thanks for enabling us to obtain effects so utterly impossible of attainment by any other means.

Collodion, as a Photographic medium, is, without doubt, far before any other. The beauty of the details obtained in good pictures, the exceeding sensibility of the medium itself, and the comparative ease of its manipulation, place it at the head of all Photographic agents.

Researches in the preparation of Collodion might appear superfluous, now that it is supplied of the best quality by so many makers; but as some persons of an independent turn of mind still prefer manufacturing their own, and as an article of uniform quality is always desirable, and it being more economical for each photographer to prepare that which he himself uses, I venture to bring forward the subject with the hope of assisting them. I yield to the temptation to give, in this place, an account of the process of manufacturing Collodion wool or gun-cotton, which I have discovered in an English work on photography; because the possession of a reliable process is desirable and quite in harmony with the purposes of this book.

HOW TO PREPARE GUN-COTTON.

Five parts, by measure, of sulphuric acid and four of nitric acid of specific gravity, not lower than 1.4, are mixed in an earthen-ware or thin glass-vessel capable of standing heat; small portions of water are added gradually (by half drachms at a time, supposing two ounces to have been mixed), testing after each addition by the immersion of a small portion of cotton. The addition of water is continued until a piece of cotton is found to contract and dissolve on immersion; when this takes place, add half the quantity of sulphuric acid previously used and (if the temperature does not exceed 130°, in which case, it must be allowed to cool to that point,) immerse as much cotton, well pulled out as can be easily and perfectly soaked; it is left in for ten minutes, taking care the mixture does not become cold. It is then transferred to cold water and thoroughly washed. This is a matter of much importance, and should be performed at first by changing the water many times, until it ceases to taste acid, and treating it then with boiling rain-water, until the color of blue litmus paper remains unchanged; the freedom from all trace of acid is insured by adding a little ammonia before the last washing. Cotton thus prepared should dissolve perfectly and instantaneously in ether containing a little alcohol, without leaving a fiber behind, and the film it produces be of the greatest strength and transparency.

Having obtained good pyroxyline by purchase, or by the above process, the next point of inquiry is with regard to the solvent; many experiments have been made to ascertain the proper proportions of ether and alcohol to produce the best Collodion, having regard to all the qualities considered necessary to a good article. As according to the definition at the head of this article, gun-cotton will dissolve in ether, it might be asked why add alcohol, and be answered by giving a variety of reasons: first, the solution in ether alone could not be sensitized, and would evaporate to dryness, or "set" so quickly as to unfit the film for immersion in the bath; as, for instance, a mixture containing one-eighth of alcohol would prove quite unfit for photographic purposes, it being almost impossible, even with the most rapid coating and immersion of the plate, to obtain a film of uniform sensitiveness and opacity throughout.

It has been found that the proportion of three parts of alcohol to five of ether produces the best results, giving without the least difficulty a film beautifully uniform and highly sensitive, and at the same time perfectly tough and easily removable from the plate if desired. These proportions are, however, more satisfactory during the season of cold weather, as it is found that the film sets too quickly in hot weather, when evaporation is so much more rapid. The surprising improvement caused by the addition of a certain quantity of alcohol, is referable to causes partly chemical and partly mechanical, for, on examining the films, it will be found in a sample containing ¼ alcohol, and occasionally, when a larger proportion is used, that on immersion in the bath the iodide of silver is formed on the surface, and can be entirely removed by friction without destroying the transparent Collodion film below, while in those Collodions containing a larger proportion of alcohol (one-half or even more) the iodide of silver is wholly in the substance, and in this state possesses the utmost of sensitiveness. This difference of condition is owing to the very sparing solubility of ether in water, which, in the first case, prevents the entrance of the nitrate of silver into the film, consequently the iodide and silver solutions meet on the surface, but on the addition of alcohol in a greater proportion, its solubility enables the two to interchange places, and thus the iodide of silver is precipitated throughout the substance of the Collodion film in a state of the utmost division.

It is most important, in the selection of ether and alcohol, to form a solvent for gun-cotton to secure that which is pure. Ether often, in fact almost always, contains alcohol, and sometimes water. Alcohol is sold as 95 per cent, which will not test higher than 85.

The quantity of alcohol contained in a sample of ether, may easily be ascertained by agitating the ether in a graduated measure-glass, (a minim glass does very well,) with half its bulk of a saturated solution of chloride of calcium. This should be poured in first, its height noticed, and the ether poured on its surface, the thumb then placed on the top, and the two shaken together; when separated, the increase of bulk acquired by the chloride of calcium indicates the quantity of alcohol present, and for this, allowance should be made in the addition of alcohol to the Collodion afterward.

Water may be detected either in alcohol or ether by allowing a drop to fall into spirits of turpentine, with which they ought to mix without turbidity—this is produced at once if they contain water. For detecting water in alcohol, benzole is a more delicate re-agent than spirits of turpentine.

A perfectly pure solvent having been secured, we shall proceed to consider the materials necessary to excite or sensitize the Collodion, so that the film, when introduced into the bath, may excite a chemical action with the nitrate of silver, producing iodide of silver, which is deposited on and in the substance of the Collodion film.

Those that are generally used are the iodides and bromides of potassium, ammonium, cadmium, and sometimes zinc and sodium; of these, all but the potassium have the great advantage of being readily soluble in any Collodion, and may, therefore, be added at once to the solution of gun-cotton, but iodide of potassium requires to be dissolved in water, and even then must be added to the alcohol before mixing with the ether, or it will be precipitated in the form of a fine powder, insoluble except by the addition of more water.

To produce a film that is best adapted to the Ferrotype-plate, it is recommended to avoid the use of potassium as an excitant; it has been found that the film of Collodion prepared with this iodide possesses too much transparency; that the smallest defect on, or discoloration of, the surface of the plate may be observed in the shadows of the picture. With a Collodion prepared with ammonium and cadmium this is not the case; the film is more opaque, and covers many defects in or on the surface of the plate. The iodides of zinc and ammonium give Collodions that are equal to any others in sensitiveness, and in gradations of tone, and in all other respects when first prepared, but after a short time they lose those good qualities to a great extent from the decomposition and liberation of free iodine, while the iodide of cadmium is a corrective of this tendency, and retains its original qualities long after the others have lost theirs.

The iodide of Cadmium, in addition to the valuable property of giving a stable Collodion, is likewise extremely soluble without being deliquescent, and being beautifully crystalline, is not liable to adulterations or impurities, and is, therefore, deserving its good reputation.

Mr. Bingham, in the "Photographic World," vol. 1, page 173, gives some formulas for the preparation of double iodides and bromides, the use of which, for exciting or salting Collodion, he very highly recommends, and which appear to me to be valuable. For the double iodide of cadmium and potassium his formula is as follows:

"Iodide of Cadmium,..........................182 grammes;
Iodide of Potassium,........................165   "
Warm water..................................300   "

Shake well and filter; then evaporate in a small evaporating dish over a slow heat.

"For ammonium and cadmium—

"Iodide of Cadmium,..........................149 grammes;
Iodide of Ammonium,........................144   "
Water (same as before.)....................   "

"Double bromides can be made as well by using these equivalents.

"The great advantage gained is, of the potassium, without any water to dissolve it, as the double iodides dissolve very readily in alcohol and ether.

"I use about the following proportions to salt my Collodion, which works soft and beautiful:

"Double Iodides,............................5 to 6 grains to oz.
Double Bromides, or
Bromide of Cadmium............2½ grains to oz.
Alcohol and Ether (equal parts)
Cotton about.............................6 grains to oz.

"I believe the double iodides to be far superior to the simple iodides. I should like to have others try them, and should like to hear what they think of them."

The two following formulas will produce the best Collodion for Ferrotypes I have ever used, and I would recommend them as worthy of trial by every Ferrotypist who shall read this book. The first I have used for fully eight years; the second I have lately adopted:

Alcohol and Ether................................5 ozs. each.
Gun-cotton, to make of suitable consist-
ency, to be immersed in Ether before
the Alcohol is added:
To every 10 ozs. of plain Collodion add
Iodide of Ammonium..........................40 grains;
Iodide of Cadmium.............................20 grains;
Bromide of Cadmium..........................20 grains.

This Collodion can be used as soon as it has settled sufficiently clear, and will keep exceedingly well. The other is equally good, but in some respects it is different, requiring more skill in its use. It is more transparent than the first, and will not, therefore, cover the defects on the surface of the plate; in fact it can not be used on plates which have been cleaned, or that are scratched or stained on the surface, whereas the first formula will produce a Collodion that will cover a multitude of defects:

> Iodide of Ammonium........................30 grains;
> Iodide of Sodium..........................10   "
> Iodide of Cadmium.........................20   "
> Bromide of Cadmium........................20   "
> Ether and Alcohol........................5 oz. each;
> Gun-cotton, (say)........................6 to 8 grs.

Or enough to make the Collodion as thick as may be, to flow evenly and smoothly over the plate.

I have found it highly beneficial to vary the proportions according to the season. During cold weather I use a greater proportion of ether, and when the weather is very warm I use less ether and more alcohol, ever varying the proportions to suit the season. In the same way it is well to use less bromide during the summer season, when the sunlight is diffused—for instance, in July and August it would be well to make up a sample thus:

> Iodide of Ammonium........................40 grains;
> Iodide of Sodium..........................10   "
> Iodide of Cadmium.........................80   "
> Bromide of Cadmium........................10   "
> Ether, (Conc.)........................... 4½ oz.
> Alcohol.................................. 5½ oz.
> Gun-cotton, (in suitable quantity)..........

It may be well to observe that caution is necessary in the use of an over proportion of alcohol, from the fact that it is likely to render the Collodion glutinous, and from its solubility in water to sooner injure the bath. During cold weather the proportions may be varied the other way without injury, except to render the Collodion less sensitive.

Having learned how to make a good quality of Collodion, it only remains that some instruction be given as to the best means of preserving and restoring Collodion to usefulness when its virtues have been destroyed by age. Those who make their own Collodion should always calculate the quantity required to last a given time. Cadmium Collodion will keep good (in a cool dark place,) for six months or more, and should it show any signs of giving out, requiring longer exposure in the camera, or should it lose its flowing qualities, it should be at once set aside and new Collodion prepared, when the old and the new may be mixed in proportions to suit with excellent results; it often appears that the mixture was better than either had been before. If a quantity of old Collodion should have collected, it may be restored by the following process:

Fill a pound bottle nearly full of the old Collodion; when it is very dark in color, you may add a few drops—three or four—of strong ammonia, and set it away to have its perfect action, which will result in restoring it to its original color—by neutralizing the acidity of the old mixture; you may then prepare say $2\frac{1}{2}$ oz. each of ether and alcohol, adding sufficient guncotton to make very thick, which you may iodize with double the number of grains to the ounce usually allowed; this mixture you may add to the old Collodion under treatment, where it will be found to work satisfactorily. It will be necessary, however, to observe while using Collodion so restored, that the bath is not deprived of its faintly acid or neutral condition by the introduction of an alkaline Collodion This may be easily guarded against by frequent testing with blue litmus paper, and the addition of a drop of pure nitric acid, always remembering that for Ferrotypes the bath should be neutral or but faintly acid; indeed, the use of acid is to be avoided, except when necessary as in such cases as the above—as, in fact, in most, if not in all cases, except when free ammonia has been added to the Collodion, the silver solution has a tendency to become acid rather than alkaline, both from the frequent presence of free iodine in the Collodion, which sets free nitric acid in the bath, and also from the slow formation of acetic acid from the alcohol and ether washed out from the plates that have been immersed.

When Collodion has become very brown or dark red in color, from excess of iodine which has been set free by long-keeping, producing the color and rendering the Collodion insensitive, it has been found that the addition of oil of cloves, in the proportion of four drops to each ounce, causes a surprising increase of sensitiveness.

The strength of the solution of nitrate of silver should be proportionate to the quantity of iodide in the Collodion, at least so far that it can not be diminished beyond a certain point (depending on the Collodion used), without a great loss of sensitiveness; or what is exactly similar, if we use a bath of a certain strength, the quantity of iodide can not be increased to any amount, but must be limited by the proportion of nitrate of silver. With a thirty-five grain solution of the latter, four grains of bromo-iodides, or iodides and bromides, answers very well; but if the quantity be increased to six grains, there is a great loss of sensitiveness, the effect being similar to that arising from an insufficient amount of alcohol in the Collodion, in consequence of the iodide of silver being deposited superficially, or even falling off the surface into the silver bath. It will be well to note here, that the formulas for Collodion herewith given require a silver solution of at least 45 grains to the ounce, and will work much better with a fifty grain solution.

By knowing the quantity of iodide contained in a Collodion, it is easy to ascertain the amount that the bath loses for each ounce, and thus to know exactly how much nitrate should be mixed to maintain the strength; thus, with a Collodion containing eight grains of iodide of ammonium to the ounce, each ounce expended removes nine and four-tenths grains of nitrate, but with iodide of potassium, the quantity removed would be slightly less.

For the purpose of pouring the Collodion over

the plates preparatory to their being immersed in the silver bath, bottles of various designs are used, some of which are patented and others are not. Most of them are designed so as to permit the Collodion to flow outward quite easily from an orifice just large enough to allow the surplus Collodion to be turned back into the bottle from the plate; this is to prevent evaporation as much as possible, while they are provided with covers instead of stoppers to keep them free from dust; hence their name, "cometless bottles." There is a bottle recently invented and patented which filters all the Collodion used, but from its liability to excessive evaporation during warm weather, its use is not recommended during that season; while for the cold season it is entirely satisfactory. The larger sizes of the "cometless bottles" are very useful, for when kept in constant use all day, there is sufficient-space in the bottom for all sediment which may form and be deposited, to remain at rest without being disturbed by the agitation incidental to flowing plates.

CHAPTER VII.

SILVER.

"This metal may be termed a photographic *sine qua non*, for it is more than probable that, but for its existence, all the interesting phenomena connected with photography would never have been observed."

Among the various metals, silver holds the second place in value and usefulness. It is also regarded as one of the noble metals, because of its resistance to the action of atmospheric air and of fire. It is described as a soft, white, metallic element, very malleable and ductile, and capable of a high polish. Its specific gravity is 10.8, or nearly eleven times as heavy as water. It occurs pure in nature, and also in combination with sulphur, arsenic, etc., and with ores of lead, copper, and gold. It is found in veins, rarely in beds, in crystalline slate rocks, gneiss, mica slate, hornblende, slate, granite, syenite, porphyry.

It is mined extensively in Norway, Sweden, Saxony, Bohemia, Hungary, Transylvania, Siberia, the Hartz, Baden, Tyrol, France, England, Chili, Peru, Mexico, and in many parts of the United States. Among the many celebrated mines of this country is the Comstock Lode, in the territory of Montana, out of which fabulous amounts are taken yearly.

Silver melts at a temperature of 1873° Fahrenheit, and at a higher temperature it burns with a reddish colored flame, and when fused by a powerful current of electricity, the flame is of a greenish cast.

This metal is so malleable and ductile that it ranks next to gold in that respect, and its tenacity is so great that it may be drawn into wire of exceeding fineness, of which lace and other delicate fabrics are made. It is capable of a most brilliant polish; the ancients used highly polished plates of silver as mirrors. For the brilliancy of polish, as well as for other high qualities, it is used in the manufacture of many articles of beauty and utility. Mixed with copper, in the proportion of $12\frac{1}{2}$ to 1, it forms the standard of British coinage.

The earliest mention of silver is in the Holy Bible, in the time of Abraham. We are not there informed of the first discovery or use of silver, either in the arts or as an article of value for exchange for other commodities as Abraham used it; so that Tubal Cain, the first worker in brass and iron, might also have been the first silversmith.

Silver as well as gold, and indeed most other metals, may be dissolved in acid; the acid being evaporated, the silver remains in a state of crystallization as a salt of silver.

The different salts of silver are obtained from the ores or from the metal itself. The

NITRATE OF SILVER

is obtained by dissolving the pure metallic silver in nitric acid, and is that salt of silver upon which all the processes of photography are founded, and beside which there is no metallic or other element by which primary photographic impressions can be made, although there are other substances which are sensitive to light. There are many processes for obtaining the pure nitrate of silver from the ore or from the metal, from among which the following is selected:

Pure nitric acid and water of equal parts should be placed in an evaporating dish over a gentle heat; when warm, add the silver. This part of the process should be carried on out of doors, or where the draft of a chimney may cause the fumes which arise to be carried off or be dissipated. After the silver is dissolved, the solution should be evaporated to dryness by a slow heat, less than will produce fusion of the salt. When the salt is dry, it should be dissolved in the least quantity of hot water; the solution should then be set aside to crystallize.

The crystallized nitrate may be purified by redissolving in pure water and allowing it to recrystallize.

Nitrate of silver thus obtained is a dry salt composed of oxide of silver and anhydrous nitric acid; its chemical symbol is (AgO, NO5), and its equivalent, therefore, 170; its combining proportion, 103; its specific gravity, 4,336.

Pure nitrate of silver is not changed by the action of light, but when it contains organic matter it soon turns black under the influence of the sun's rays. Water will dissolve its equal weight of silver, but a less proportion is capable of being dissolved in alcohol.

If any substance, such as wood, ivory, cloth, paper or a photographer's finger is first wet with a solution of silver, and then exposed to sunlight, the substance will be stained black, which stain is metallic silver, reduced by the action of the light, which will become apparent on burnishing the stain on the wood or ivory. This black stain is insoluble in all common fluids, and is on this account made the basis of indellible inks. The best ink of the kind is made by dissolving an infinitesmal portion of silver in gum-water, at the time when required for use, when it can be applied to a smooth surface with a pen; upon exposure to the light, it will turn black in and through the fiber of the material marked by this truly indellible ink.

Nitrate of silver is also used in the composition of hair-dyes, and by photographers it is frequently used involuntarily as a dye for clothes.

Nitrate of silver is precipitated from solution, by salts of iron, copper, zinc, etc., in the form of a metallic powder—with bicarbonate of soda it is precipitated as a carbonate of silver.

When desirable to reduce silver from a solution to a metallic state, the quickest and best way is to measure the solution, and put in a wide-mouth bottle or into an evaporating dish, and for every fifty ounces of solution add three ounces of sulphuric acid, and three ounces of clean zinc in strips—iron, if more convenient, would answer the same purpose—the zinc or iron should be placed in the silver solution first, and then the acid part at a time; this part of the process should be done out of doors, or in a strong draft, to carry off the horrible fumes which arise; the precipitate forms rapidly on the zinc, and should from time to time be rubbed or scraped off. As soon as ebullition ceases, add more acid; at the last, it is well to test the solution to ascertain if the operation is complete, which can be done by taking a small quantity of the solution, a test-tube, and add a drop or two of hydrocloric acid, or a pinch of common salt; if a white precipitate is formed, there still remains silver in the solution, to reduce which add more acid and clean the zinc.

After the silver has been precipitated, remove the remaining pieces of zinc or iron, and allow the sediment to settle, after which pour off the liquid, and wash the precipitate two or three times with clean water until blue litmus paper ceases to turn red in the liquid, each time allowing the sediment to fall to the bottom before decanting the liquid.

You have now in the washed precipitate a grayish powder, which is comparatively pure metallic silver, which, if you choose, may be converted into solution again by adding nitric acid sufficient to re-dissolve, or the precipitate may be dried and placed in a crucible with a small quantity of nitrate of potash, and fused; the potash will remove any trace of iron or zinc. I have by this method converted an old and useless solution of silver into a good working bath in a very short time, although it is better not to do it in a hurry.

Nitrate of silver may also be reduced from solution by evaporating to dryness; at the last, the heat should be very gentle, because in the presence of organic matter the nitrate is easily changed to pure silver, which would require to be re-dissolved.

The fused mass presents a yellowish appearance, and readily dissolves in water, leaving the organic matter and residues of cadmium and potassium in a thick, pasty mass of a dark color, but which also contains some silver, and on that account should be saved with other wastes.

It has been said that the fusion of the residues of photographer's old silver solutions is attended with some danger from the not improbable formation of fulminating silver, a most powerfully explosive compound. Some idea of its explosive force may be obtained from one of Charles Reade's novels.

The solution of nitrate of silver used by photographers for the preparation of sensitized surfaces, or surfaces rendered sensitive to the action of light by the deposition thereon, upon immersion in the silver solution of certain salts of silver, such as iodides or bromides of that metal, is the most important solution claiming the attention of the photographer.

The formulas for the preparation of such a solution are almost innumerable, and they are as diverse as are the minds of their authors or inventors, and it would appear that minds of no ordinary inventive powers have been engaged in such labors, judging from published formulas, which may be found in every library of photographic works.

The preparation of a silver solution or bath, however, is a matter of no small importance, as upon its successful operation depends all the interests of the establishment. The perfect operation of the silver bath is a matter of primary importance to the operator, no matter how it may be prepared, or by what formula.

There are various methods used in the preparation of nitrate of silver by manufacturing chemists—each one may have his own favorite process. One firm may take pleasure in producing a quality that shall be remarkable for the beauty and size of its crystals; another, for the peculiar whiteness and seeming purity of their product, while yet another may pride themselves upon a high stàndard of purity, regardless of the size of the crystal, or of the whiteness and brilliancy thereof. The latter we would recommend wherever he may be found, and having ascertained by fair trial the purity of such a manufacture of silver, ever continue to use the same. Avoid change, because of the uncertainty which must surely follow. Every change must partake of the nature of an experiment, and experiments should be conducted separately.

The quality of the nitrate of silver having been ascertained and decided on, the next thing to be considered is the purity of the water used, in which the nitrate is to be dissolved. One will recommend distilled water for absolute purity; another says rain-water is pure enough, while others contend that ice-water is better than either of the foregoing. This is a matter that might well be left to the decision of each individual for himself. Water may be tested for purity by dissolving a few grains of nitrate of silver in a small quantity of the water about to be used, when, if the water remains clear, and there is no deposit thrown down, the indications are in favor of its purity; but if a gray or whitish deposit takes place, or the water changes its color to a white or milky appearance, it is not pure.

In the preparation of a solution of silver for a

bath it is always best to procure the purest water, but in the absence of such, or when distilled, rain, or ice-water can not be procured, the operations of the gallery need not cease.

The proper course to pursue in this case, would be to take the water that is used for ordinary purposes, and proceed as follows: In ½ gallon of water, dissolve 4 ounces nitrate of silver, and add 2 grains of iodide of potassium. Shake well, and set in the sunshine for three or four hours—one hour of clear sunshine is sufficient—after which filter and strengthen as desired.

Forty-five grains of nitrate to the ounce of water gives the most satisfactory results. The bath is now ready for use, and in most cases will work as perfectly as it ever will. Should it, however, not work satisfactorily, coat a plate of glass with Collodion and immerse in the bath; allow it to remain there a few minutes, after which, if the bath still refuses satisfactory results, add a few drops of pure nitric acid, when you will find all difficulties to have disappeared, and the bath will work splendidly.

If the Collodion recommended in this book be used with the bath made as above, it will remain in good condition until it has been greatly reduced in strength, and shall have become so saturated with alcohol and ether as to render it quite difficult to flow the developer, when it will be quite proper to replace with a new or fresh bath, which should always be kept on hand ready for use.

We will now inquire into the condition of the solution just relieved from duty, and ascertain what is necessary to be done to again fit it for use.

First, then, the solution contains among its disturbing elements both alcohol and ether in excess, which it received in small quantities from each plate that has been immersed, and the presence of which is indicated by a slower operation of the bath in coating the plate; and in the operation of developing, by the difficulty experienced in flowing the developer evenly and smoothly over the plate.

The solution may also contain iodide of silver in excess, called free iodide, which it also receives in minute quantities from the sensitized Collodion with which the plates are coated before immersion in the bath. The Collodion contains iodide, which, upon the introduction of the plate into the silver solution, immediately combines with the silver to form an iodide of silver upon and in the collodionized surface; in this operation, portions of iodine escape, and combining with the silver, is held in solution in the bath until such time as a greater quantity has been received than can be held in solution, when the character of the iodide changes from a state of solution to that of suspension, in which state, innumerable small particles or atoms of iodide of silver are floating in and through the solution. Free iodide in the bath is indicated by pin-holes in negatives, and by a rough and sanded appearance of the plate when removed from the bath, and by being covered by black spots when developed.

The solution may also contain an excess of organic matter, the presence of which is indicated by a tendency to fog in the development, and by an absence of transparency in the shadows, to counteract which pure nitric acid is used. The acid holds the organic matter in solution, but it has also the evil effect of hastening the accumulation of the cause of the first difficulty, by attacking the edges and unprotected portions of the plates, and by taking up and holding in solution such particles of organic matter as may collect in and upon the surface of the bath dish. For this reason, the use of nitric acid in the bath, except in cases where it is absolutely necessary, should be discountenanced.

We find, then, that our old solution is burdened with a number of evil qualities, which we will proceed to dispose of, and casting out, restore the solution to its pristine purity. For that purpose, we will add to the solution sufficient carbonate of soda or concentrated ammonia to counteract the acid, barely enough to prevent the change of color in litmus paper from blue to red when immersed in the solution. We will now pour into an evaporating, or other dish, four fluid ounces of water, into which we will pour the half-gallon more, or less, of solution; the effect is to change the transparency of the solution to a dense milky whiteness, which is iodide of silver, set free by reducing the strength of the solution. This should now be filtered to remove the iodide, after which it should be returned to the evaporating dish, and set over a fire, and boiled down to less than the original quantity; this will effectually remove, by evaporation, the alcohol and ether. There will, also, during the process of boiling down, be deposited a black, muddy sediment, which is partly iodide of silver and partly organic matter. The solution should be then diluted with cold water enough to restore to the original quantity, poured into a white glass bottle, and set in the sunshine for a day, or until it is again required for use, when it should be strengthened by adding fresh nitrate of silver, to restore it to the standard strength of 45 grains to the ounce fluid.

During the summer season, when the sun is bright and warm, it is not necessary to boil the bath solution to remove the alcohol and ether. The bath, when unfit for further use, should be neutralized and set in the sunshine, after being diluted with sufficient water to restore it to its original bulk. It will be well to notice that, in diluting or adding water to an old bath, the water should not be poured into the bath, but the bath solution should be poured into the dish containing the water it is intended to add, the effect of which is to set free a greater quantity of the iodide of silver. By pouring the bath solution into the water, the first part of the solution is compelled to give up all or nearly all of its iodide, while the last to go in will have to part with as much in proportion as would the whole, if the water had been added to the solution.

The heat of the sun will cause the ether and alcohol to evaporate from the solution, which, being free from acid, the particles of organic matter are no longer held in solution, in which state the light could have no effect; but being in suspension, and being saturated with silver, the light falling upon and passing through them, causes a chemical change to take place in the innumerable particles or atoms, the nitrate or iodide of silver they contain is changed into a metallic state, or into some other combination, by which they become heavier and fall to the bottom.

The appearance of the solution during this process is altogether changed from a total absence of color to a light red, then a darker shade, and then quite black; the black particles then fall to the bottom, and the solution becomes once more colorless. When required for use, it should be strengthened, and is then ready.

During the season of cold weather, it is necessary, in order to remove the alcohol, to boil the solution, as evaporation by sun heat at that season of the year would be a slow process. After filtering such a solution the filter should be preserved for the Silver which is contained therein. All other wastes of the dark-room, such as cloths for wiping holders, paper on which plates are drained when taken from the bath, and every thing which has any trace of Silver upon it should be kept in a receptacle for the purpose, and after the collection of a sufficient quantity should be treated for the recovery of the Silver.

The loss of Silver in washing pictures after development, and in the waste of the solution of cyanide of potassium, in which they are cleared or fixed, may be prevented by having a water-tight box or barrel, which will hold all the water likely to be used in a day's work, placed under the water faucet. Every evening a quantity of solution of common sulphate of iron should be thrown into the water, and in the morning the water should be drawn off by a syphon, leaving room for another day's work, when the same process may be repeated. This apparatus costs very little infringes no patent, and will save in proportion to the amount of business done from one to many pounds of Silver each year.

Much silver may be saved from the developing of plates by performing that operation over a large funnel in which may be placed a loose cotton filter, or, what is better, an old felt hat may be used, by tacking the rim to a frame; the solution will filter through, leaving all the Silver washed from the surface of the plate. The developer may be received below in a wide-mouth bottle, and can be used again with great advantage in the proportion of two parts of old to one of new. After using the bat for a year, the deposit which remains, and is nearly all metallic silver, may be recovered by the proper means.

Every precaution should be taken against the waste of Silver; time and money can not be better invested than in devising and procuring appliances for saving the Silver which would otherwise be lost in the water that runs from your dark-room sink. When it is taken into consideration that of all the Silver used in photographic establishments, in making positives and negatives, not more than ten per cent. of the whole remains in the finished picture, either positive or negative, an idea may be formed of the amount that passes into the sewers, unless intercepted before it reaches the pipes conducting thereto. This great waste of precious metal has no excuse, neither can there be any excuse for it, and, therefore, it claims and is receiving more attention year by year; in fact, in the larger cities every gallery has its apparatus for saving the Silver

Two gentlemen have become famous among photographers by the attempted enforcement of a patent which they claimed for recovering the salts of silver from solution. Their claim covered every known means of precipitation of nitrate of silver from solution.

THE FERROTYPE.

GLASS BATH.—To hold the Nitrate of Silver solution, nothing can be so surely depended upon for chemical purity as glass. No other description of bath dish affords the same advantages. The most desirable dish is the "solid glass," of which sizes from 6. by 8. to 14. by 20. inches, are neatly inclosed in light wooden boxes, with hinged covers, to exclude light and dust. These bath dishes are, however, quite expensive, and this to the ferrotypist who makes pictures for profit, is a very important consideration. They are also, unfortunately, very liable to break, and the breakage of one of these baths, especially when filled with silver solution, is no laughing matter.

There is another quality of glass bath which is made of pieces of plate glass, cemented together with marine glue or other substance capable of resisting the action of silver solution, and incased solidly with wood. These also are expensive, and are very heavy.

Another and less expensive bath dish has lately been adopted in some galleries. It is a light box of suitable shape, made of clear pine, free from knots or blemishes, the pieces joined with either asphaltum, coal tar, or pitch, and screwed firmly together. The box, when complete, is filled with hot coal tar, such as is used for roofing, and after a time is emptied and allowed to dry. The edges of the cover and the top of the box are carefully saturated with the tar, and when thoroughly dry are varnished, and the box is then fit for use, and is, when properly made, cheap, durable, and efficient.

It is not considered necessary to describe the qualities of porcelain, rubber, or photographic-ware baths, as their good qualities are few and their bad qualities are not properly describable. The bath dish should always be scrupulously clean, and when in use should be kept covered. When the solution requires filtering, the dish should be cleaned with a swab, to remove the sediment from the bottom and sides.

CHAPTER VIII.

DEVELOPER AND DEVELOPMENT.

Proto-Sulphate of Iron as a Developer.

The developing solution, is an aqueous solution of iron with acid, and sometimes alcohol. The form in which iron can be used as a developing agent is that of a crystalized salt. This salt, often termed copperas or green vitriol, is a substance formed in abundant quantities, and is used for a variety of purposes in the arts. Commercial sulphate of iron, however, being prepared on a large scale, requires re-crystallization to render it sufficiently pure for photographic purposes.

Pure sulphate of iron occurs in the form of large transparent crystals, of a delicate green color. By exposure to the air they gradually absorb oxygen, and become rusty on the surface. The sulphate of iron, colorless at first, afterward changes to a red tint, and deposits a brown powder. This powder is basic persulphate of iron; that is, a persulphate containing an excess of oxide or base. By the addition of acetic acid to the solution, the formation of a deposit is prevented, the brown powder being soluble in acid liquids.

The action of sulphate of iron upon the nitrate of silver solution is to change its character by converting the silver of the solution to a metallic state, in which state it is deposited in the form of a grayish powder, the character of the deposit being somewhat affected by the acid.

Various acids are used in the developing solution. The most prominent are acetic, glacial acetic, nitric, citric, gallic, and pyrogallic acids. The last three, however, are more used in the process of re-development of negatives. The first is, for many reasons, the best, and is generally used in solutions for the primary development of negatives and always for positives.

Acetic acid is a product of the oxydation of alcohol. Spirituous liquors when perfectly pure are not affected by exposure to the air, but if a portion of yeast or nitrogenious organic matter of any kind be added it soon acts as a *ferment*, and causes the spirit to unite with oxygen derived from the atmosphere, and so to become *sour* from the formation of acetic acid or vinegar. Acetic acid is also produced on a large scale by heating wood in a close vessel. A substance distills over, which is acetic acid contaminated with empyreumatic and tarry matter; it is termed pyroligneous acid, and is much used in commerce.

The most concentrated acetic acid may be obtained by neutralizing common vinegar with carbonate of soda, and crystallizing out the acetate of soda so formed. This acetate of soda is then distilled with sulphuric acid, which removes the soda, and liberates acetic acid, which, being volatile, distills over and may be condensed.

The use of acetic acid in the developing solution, besides its preservative effect upon the solution itself, is for the purpose of retarding the action of the iron in the reduction of the salts of silver to a metallic state, also favorably affecting the character of the deposit. Alcohol is used in the developing solution for the purpose of causing it to flow evenly and smoothly over the surface of the plate.

When new silver is used for coating the plate, the developer requires no alcohol, but as every plate which is immersed in the silver solution imparts to it a portion of ether and alcohol from the collodion film, the silver bath soon acquires enough to change somewhat the character of the sensitized surface, giving it the power to repel the developing solution. By the addition of alcohol to the developing solution this repelling power is overcome.

We will now describe the process of development. The correct definition of the last word of the title at the head of this article, according to Webster, is, "The act of developing or disclosing that which is unknown," and beautifully describes one of the wonderful processes of our art.

A ferro-plate is coated with collodion and immersed in a solution of nitrate of silver. After being allowed to remain a few minutes, it is removed and placed in the shield or plate-holder. This operation must be done in a dark chamber, or in one the light of which is of non-actinic character; for so sensitive is the plate on being removed from the bath, that the smallest ray of white or actinic light falling upon it, leaves its mark. The plate when removed from the bath is found to be changed in appearance; the glossy black surface no longer shows through the transparent collodion film, but, instead, a beautiful creamy opacity hides the surface from view. The plate-holder is now taken to the camera and exposed to the action of light reflected from some object animate or inanimate; after which it is again removed to the dark chamber. If now it be subjected to the most careful examination, no visible change can be noted. It has the same rich yellowish white color, and is as opaque as before. A very important change has, however, taken place in the character, if not in the appearance, of the surface, which change can only be made apparent to the eye, and the chemical action of light on the sensitized film can only be made known through the action of the developing solution in the process of development.

The plate may now be removed from the holder, and being held by the left hand between the thumb and fore-finger, the other fingers acting as a brace to support it and keep it steady, a solution is poured gently but quickly upon the end and corner nearest the hand, and caused to flow evenly over the whole surface of the plate, without allowing it to rest at any part until the whole is covered; and for that purpose the plate should be held so as to incline downward, and always away from the holder. After the whole surface shall have been covered, the solution should be caused to flow backward and forward, by gently rocking the plate, taking care not to allow any of the solution to run off, either when pouring on or afterward, until the process is complete.

The solution will hardly have covered the plate before an image will begin to be developed, at first slowly, then quicker and more plainly it will appear, until in a short time the perfect image will stand out boldly, when the development is complete.

It is the process of development, and the chemical and other changes which take place under the action of the developing solution, which it is desired to explain and make clear to the intelligence of the reader.

First, then, we will try to explain the chemical action which takes place in the sensitized collodion film, when exposed in the camera. The collodion plate, upon being taken from the silver bath, has received in and on its surface a deposit, more or less dense, of iodide of silver, which, upon being exposed in the camera to the action of light reflected from an inanimate object or from a person sitting for a portrait, is converted to a sub-iodide by the loss of oxygen, chlorine, etc.;

or as it is otherwise explained, the iodide of silver contains a portion of oxygen, which it is known has but litte affinity with the noble metals. By the action of light the iodide of silver is caused to give off a portion or all of its oxygen, and the silver with which it was combined is at once reduced to a metallic state, but in so small a proportion as not to affect the appearance of the plate to the eye.

The change that has taken place, then, is that the image of the sitter is impressed on the sensitized film, the light parts, such as the face, hands, and parts of the clothing reflecting light; by a change of the iodide of silver to a metallic state, the dark portions, such as hair, eyes and shadows of the dress having no effect, or very little if any, upon the film.

The plate being now taken to the developing stand, the developer, an aqueous solution of iron with acid, is flowed upon it, the effect being that the iron and acid act upon the nitrate of silver with which the plate is still wet, and causes a deposit of pure metallic silver upon all parts of the surface which is prepared to receive it, which parts are those that have been touched by light and have been converted into a metallic state, so that the development causes a greater deposit of metallic silver upon those parts only where metallic silver has been formed by the action of light. At this stage, when the development is complete, we find that all portions of the plate that have not felt the action of light, remain as opaque as before exposure, and with very little if any change of color, remaining in the same state as when taken from the bath, that is, iodide of silver; but the image, which now stands out plainly, is composed of metallic silver in the light and intermediate part, and iodide of silver in the shadows. If the plate is now immersed in a solution of cyanide of potassium (which is a powerful solvent of the iodide of silver), it will at once be dissolved and removed, leaving the image, which is in the light parts metallic silver, in the dark parts the black surface of the plate showing through the collodion film; so that the action of light in the camera is to produce on the surface of the sensitized plate, an image of the object in focus in metallic silver, which serves as a basis upon which to deposit more metallic silver in the process of development. And as metallic silver in this process will not deposit itself except upon a metallic surface, we can easily understand why an image may not be developed upon an under exposed plate, as the exposure will not have been of sufficient duration to have formed a basis. An over-exposure, in like manner, will have destroyed the proper gradations by extending the primary change into the shadows.

The development of the latent image comes second only in importance to the posing and lighting of the subject preparatory to the exposure of the plate, to which I concede the first place only for the reason that if the lighting is faulty and the position is bad, the best development will not make a good picture.

The whole treatment of this manipulation demands from the operator a judicious appreciation of the nature of the subject—the time of exposure, the temperature, the nature of the component parts of the developing solution, and the exercise of a good judgment, a quick eye, and a steady hand. In fact, very great importance attaches itself to every particular of this process, as much to the quality of the materials used as to their true proportions and harmonious effect; all of which is particularly true of the development of Ferrotypes, for upon this process depends all the brilliancy, the beauty, tone, and all that makes the picture desirable.

In the preparation of a developing solution for Ferrotypes, we must first consider that we desire to produce a different effect in the positive picture from what is requisite in a negative; that the effects we want in the positive would be undesirable in a negative, and, therefore, the solution that would develop a negative properly would be unsuitable for a Ferrotype, and *vice versa*.

The Ferrotype, to be admired, must be full of detail, as much so as the negative. The shadows, also, should be as transparent and clear, but the lights should be pure and as white as the pure silver will make them; for upon the purity of the high lights and the transparency of the shadows depends the brilliancy of the pictures, that quality which above all others makes the Ferrotype the rival of the Daguerreotype. The proper solution for developing Ferrotypes is the one which will produce these effects in the highest degree, and will also produce the most satisfactory effects with the greatest certainty, with the possibility of its modification to suit the ever varying exigencies of the dark room.

It has always been the good fortune of the writer to find the most encouraging results proceeding from the simplest causes, or, in other words, the simplest processes in the every-day work of the gallery produced invariably the best results—probably because where there are a few things to learn and understand properly, they can be better learned and more thoroughly understood than when there are many.

The formula for developing solution, given below, will be found by careful trial every thing that can be desired for Ferrotypes, and it is hoped that it will, if adopted for use, be always used as directed:

Water...64 oz.
Protosulphate of Iron............................. 4 "
Acetic Acid... 4 "
Alcohol.. 4 "

The four ounces of iron should be put into a loose filter, and the water filtered through, which will dissolve the iron readily. The acetic acid need not be added until required for use. The alcohol need not be added at all, if the solution flows readily on the plate; it is, however, better to add it at once to make sure.

To use the solution, the proper way is to develop over a funnel large enough to receive all the waste solution that may run off the plate in flowing, allowing it to filter through cotton into a bottle below, being careful always to drain the plate under development of all surplus solution before the development is complete, so that all the solution will be saved, and being filtered free from the silver taken up during the development, falls into the bottle below and is ready for use again, which may be done by adding two-thirds of the old solution to one-third of the new. It will be seen that, in order to use so large a proportion of the old solution, it will be necessary that at least two-thirds of all that is used should fall into the filter, but by giving attention to the directions above a larger proportion can very easily be saved. By this process we obtain a solution that will produce the best chemical effects in the Ferrotype, with the least outlay for materials, for it will be seen that we are using only one-third the quantity of new solution that would otherwise be expended, so that if Ferrotypes are made for profit, here is a large saving, which is a profit, of two-thirds of the ordinary expense for developing materials.

This solution may also be modified to suit all degrees of temperature, and all periods of exposure, by varying the proportions of old and new. If we have given too much time in exposure, we may weaken the solution with the old; if too short an exposure has been made, we strengthen with new. If it is desired to produce a white ground and purer high lights, the plate may be flowed with a small portion of the old unfiltered, which gives a heavy deposit of silver; this, however, should not be done until after the plate is partially developed by the ordinary solution.

An excellent filter has been before described, but is worthy of more careful attention in this connection. A soft felt hat may be stretched on a frame, or placed in a large glass funnel, over which to develop all pictures; the surplus solution falling into the hat is more perfectly filtered, and the deposit which remains in the filter, after enough shall have collected to interfere with its usefulness, being all silver, may be recovered in a metallic state by any of the processes usually employed for that purpose, among which the following will be found the most economical, and, perhaps, within the means and ability of a greater number than would by any other process:

The residue may be taken from the filter, and placed in a porcelain evaporating dish containing a solution composed of equal parts of nitric acid and water; the whole should be gently heated until the action of the acid has ceased, when the heat may be increased, and the product evaporated to dryness; it may then, again, be dissolved in water, converted into a metallic state by the process described in the article on silver, and re-converted into nitrate.

This process will give a perfectly pure nitrate of silver, and is probably the most economical and certain in its results of all the different methods for recovering silver from photographic wastes.

It is recommended that the process of development should be carefully studied by the Ferrotypist, principally because so much of the success of the establishment depends on the production of a brilliant and pleasing pictorial effect, which, in turn, depends on the development, so that a habit of noting every varying phase of the process, and of applying corrections here, accelerants there, and checks and aids wherever required, will be found of incalculable advantage.

This constant watchfulness might well be extended to and include every manipulation and every process that goes to the production of the picture; but nowhere else is it so necessary, and in no other place will it result in so much good, as in the dark-room, while watching the appearance of the image as it emerges from obscurity and nothingness; for here we have under our observation the plate; we are to judge at this time, the sufficiency of the coating of iodide derived from the bath, of the time of exposure, whether too long or too short, of the propriety of the lighting and posing, and of the action of the developing solution; in every particular of which there is an endless variation which taxes every power of the mind, and the study of which is an endless source of pleasure and excitement. It is well, also, to accustom the eye to note, and the mind to judge of the strength of light passing through the lens, and thrown on the ground or object-glass, so that it will not be necessary to guess at the proper time of exposure. This may be made a matter of certainty by a course of careful observation, and of noting all mistakes, and remembering all successes.

In this connection, I am tempted to give expression to a feeling of contempt which I have always felt for mere guess-work in this or any other art or business. It betokens the lack of that careful habit of study and observation, without which no considerable degree of success can ever be attained. What would be said of the watchmaker, to whom you had taken your watch, if he could not indicate the exact nature and cause of the stoppage or the variation you wished corrected? So of the Ferrotypist, if he could not tell wherein his picture was defective, and had not the ability to apply the proper remedy. Of course, all this must be acquired, but it can never be acquired without much pains-taking study. Again, I say to the Ferrotypist,

>Observe, and remember!
>Experiment, and remember!
>If you make a mistake, remember!
>Or are successful, remember!
>*Remember every thing!*

FIXING SOLUTION.—A bath dish of the same size as that used for the silver solution, large enough to take the largest plate exposed, should be used for the cyanide of potassium, or fixing solution; the plates should be fixed or cleared up by dipping them into the solution in the same manner as the collodionized plates are immersed in the silver bath. The cyanide dish should always be covered, to avoid the deleterious fumes which arise from that solution, and it is for this reason, as well as its greater convenience, that such a bath dish is recommended.

Rubber dippers are the best for both the silver and the fixing solutions, as the vulcanized rubber has no appreciable effect on either.

CYANIDE OF POTASSIUM, AND ITS USE AS A FIXING SOLUTION.—The sensitized plate having been exposed, and the image developed, it requires to pass through yet further treatment to render the image indestructible by light. It is true that the developed image is permanent, but it is surrounded by, and contains in its shadows, the unchanged iodide and other salts of silver, which, upon exposure to light, would be decomposed by its action, and the picture would be thus lost or rendered useless. It is, therefore, necessary to remove this salt by applying some chemical agent capable of dissolving it.

Cyanide of potassium is a compound of cyanogen gas with the metal potassium. Cyanogen is not an elementary body, like chlorin or iodine, but consists of carbon and nitrogen united in a peculiar manner. Although a compound substance, it reacts in the manner of an element, and is, therefore, an exception to the ordinary laws of chemistry.

The cyanide of potassium is the salt most frequently employed in fixing. It occurs in commerce in the form of fused lumps of considerable size; in this state, it is usually contaminated with a large percentage of carbonate of potash, amounting in some cases to more than half its weight. By boiling in proof spirit, the cyanide may be extracted and crystallized, but this operation is scarcely required, as far as its use in photography is concerned.

Cyanide of potassium absorbs moisture on exposure to the air, and is very soluble in water, but the solution decomposes on keeping, changing in color, and evolving the odor of *prussic acid*, which is a cyanide of hydrogen. Cyanide of potassium is highly poisonous, and should, therefore, be used with caution.

Solution of cyanide of potassium is a most energetic agent in dissolving the insoluble silver salts; far more so in proportion to the quantity used, than the hyposulphate of soda. The salts are in all cases converted into cyanides, and exist in the solution in the form of soluble double salts, which, unlike the double iodides, are not affected by dilution with water. Cyanide of potassium is unadapted for the fixing of positive proofs upon chloride of silver, and even when a developer has been used, as in the case of a Ferrotype, unless the solution is tolerably dilute, it is likely to attack the image and destroy it.

CHAPTER IX.

THE COLLODION PROCESS.

HAVING made the reader familiar with the various instruments and apparatus which are used in the glass or operating room, and given complete directions for the preparation of the various solutions used in the dark chamber, explained their nature and properties, and the purposes for which they are used, it now remains to describe the various manipulations necessary for the production of a picture by the Collodion process. In the first place, we will imagine that the operator, having every thing in complete readiness for the day's work, is waiting for his first morning customer. The reception-room has been nicely swept; the various articles of furniture have been neatly dusted and disposed around the room with an eye to effect. The pictures on the walls are free from dust, the glass cleaned, and every object in the room showing care and attention. A lady enters. She looks around the walls, sees that neatness and order are apparent in the arrangement of the furniture and in the care of the room. She at once feels that she has come to the right place; that the taste and skill exhibited in the placing of a chair, or in the arrangement of a table or a show-case, in the reception room, will not be lacking in the more important requirements of the pose, choice of view, illumination, or lighting of the subject, or in any of the various operations of the glass-room in which the possession of good taste and a knowledge of the principles of art are so very necessary, and give to the possessor so many advantages.

You immediately become aware, on entering into conversation with the lady, that a good impression has been made, and that she has had a feeling of confidence inspired within her by the appearance of the surroundings. She is unreserved, makes her wishes known in a frank and liberal manner, and, being met with courtesy and attention, she gives her order. She intended to have one card Ferrotype made to send to a friend, but she likes the attention bestowed upon her and the samples of work shown her, and decides to take half a dozen instead of one. If you do a large business, you immediately fill out a blank with her order, and the amount it will come to, doing it plainly, and passing it to her in such a manner that she may take notice of the order and the price, requesting her, at the same time, to give it to the operator or artist in the glass-room when he is about to make her picture. This is for the purpose, in the first place, of systematizing business. All orders should be given at the desk or appropriate place in the reception-room. The orders should be written on checks or tickets, with the amount in money plainly exhibited in figures, so that there may be no misunderstanding in regard to the price, and it will also be a hint to pay in advance, which, in my opinion, ought never to be insisted upon, however desirable it is; the hint, in a majority of cases, is sufficient, the money is paid, when the ticket is marked "paid," and, being numbered, secures the lady a sitting in her turn. You politely request the lady to prepare for her sitting, showing her to the dressing-room, making what explanations may be necessary for her guidance.

We now pass to the dark-room, where we find the next part of the process is carried on, that of coating the plates with collodion, and then immersing them in a silver bath. We select a plate of the desired size, see that the surface is flat, brush it carefully with a wide, soft brush, to free it from dust which may have settled on the surface, and holding it firmly between the thumb and fore-finger of the left hand, the remaining finger acting as a brace to support and steady the plate, we pour from the bottle, held in the right hand, a portion of collodion upon the end or part of the plate farthest from the fingers, allowing it to flow gently over the plate and toward the left lower corner, and thence to the right-hand lower corner, where we allow the collodion to flow off the plate into the bottle held in the right hand. As soon as the collodion has commenced to flow from the plate, it should be turned first to the side and then to the end, or *vice versa*, so that the collodion film may be even and smooth; for if it is allowed to flow off the plate steadily in one direction, there would appear a series of lines or ridges in the direction of the flow, but by tilting the plate the direction of this flow is changed, and these lines are destroyed. This is of much importance, an even and homogeneous film being necessary to the production of a good picture. After the collodion has ceased to flow from the plate into the bottle, the latter should be set on the shelf or stand and covered, after which the plate is changed from the left to the right hand, all this time being kept in motion, until the film has set; that is, become hard enough to break when touched by the point of the finger, on the corner from which the surplus collodion was allowed to run. As soon as it has become firm and dry enough (by the evaporation of ether from the surface,) to bear the touch of the finger, without flowing over the place touched, it is ready to be immersed in the silver bath, where it is allowed to remain about two minutes, or until the surface has become coated with iodide of silver. When it is withdrawn it presents a smooth yellowish white appearance. Should there appear on the surface oily lines in the direction of the dip, the surface is not sufficiently coated and should again be placed in the bath; and if necessary to hasten the action of the bath, the plate may be moved about a few seconds, when it will be found to have become smoothly and evenly coated. It may now be taken from the dipper and placed in the plate-holder or shield, after it has been held over the bath long enough to allow the surplus solution to run off. The plate-holder is now to be taken to the camera stand and placed in its appropriate rest, until the pose of the sitter can be made and the proper illumination secured. For directions as to the illumination position, etc., etc., I would direct the reader to the chapter under that head on page 171.

It is proper, prior to seating the subject, to ask if there is any favorite position or style which would be preferred. If not, it devolves on the artist to decide as to the proper size of the head, the portion of the figure to be taken, the best view of the face, the best illumination to bring out good points and to hide defects, and to devise means to secure good expressions, all of which having been done, the camera is placed in proper condition, and the ground glass in the rear adjusted. The correct focus is next to be secured. To this end a cloth, which is kept for the purpose, is thrown over the camera and the head, shutting out all the light from the object-glass, enabling us to see the image of the sitter, in an inverted position, on the glass. The focus is adjusted by moving the lens with the right hand from or toward the object-glass, until the correct focus is found, which is the place of most perfect definition.

Plenty of time should be devoted to the adjustment of the focus. The operator should always make a perfect certainty of securing a good focus. If it is found that parts of the figure project too far forward, or otherwise, to include them in the range of the instrument, the position should be changed so as to bring all parts of the figure into such a position (consistent with ease and grace) as to secure a distinct image, every part of which shall be equally sharp in definition on the ground glass. The plate-holder may now be pushed into position, or, as in some boxes, the ground glass may be removed and the plate-holder placed in the position it had occupied, the lens being first covered with a cap provided with each lens for that purpose, or by the cloth used in focusing. After the plate-holder is in position, the sitter is directed to look toward some object. Some remarks may be made about expression, or any little alteration of position or of the arrangement of the drapery, before the impression is secured. It is well, just previous to the removal of the cover from the lens, to review the sitter, taking note of the way the light falls, and the effect on the drapery and face, and to make at this time, in as rapid a manner as possible, any changes which may suggest themselves to the mind. Every thing being ready, the slide of the plate-holder is drawn out, the hand is placed on the cap or cover of the lens, and with a cautionary word always spoken, so as to make a pleasant expression or to pleasingly affect the sitter, the cover is removed and the exposure of the plate commenced, to continue as long as it may be considered necessary. And in this part of the manipulations the mind should be accustomed, by a system of careful observations, to judge correctly, from the illumination of the image on the object-glass, as to the time necessary for the action of the light on the sensitive plate. Great proficiency may be attained in this important part of the business by careful attention and observation. The time necessary for the exposure of the plate having elapsed, the cover is replaced on the lens and the slide of the plate-holder returned to its proper position, and the holder removed and taken to the dark-room, placed on its stand or rest, the door at the back opened, and the plate taken out on the left hand by turning the holder with the right hand, so that it will fall out. If it is a large plate, the glass (which was at the back of it in the holder) is now taken in the left hand, the plate resting on it. The operator turns to the developing stand, and taking the bottle containing the developing solution in the right hand, a portion of its contents is poured over the surface of the plate; or, rather, as this is a very nice operation, the solution is poured on the extreme corner nearest the right hand, or on the end or side of the plate next the right hand, and by a quick but steady motion of the left hand the solution is caused to flow over the whole surface of the plate without stopping, allowing none, or as little as possible, to run off the opposite edge of the plate. This operation is a difficult one at first, but by careful practice the necessary skill is easily acquired. The plate, while the developing operation is going on, should be kept in motion, to cause the solution to flow backward and forward over the surface; or when the solution flows reluctantly, the plate may be taken between both hands and violently agitated in a horizontal direction, care being taken to retain all the solution on its surface until the image is brought out distinctly, and all the folds of the drapery begin to show. Careful attention must be given to the general appearance of the image at this stage, and particularly to the high lights, contrasting them with the shadows of the hair, the projections of the face, and the drapery. A little practice gives one the ability to decide when the development has proceeded far enough. Just before this point has been arrived at, the surplus developer which remains upon plate is allowed to drain into the funnel over which the operation has been performed, for a second or two after which the image must be watched, as the development still goes on; and when sufficiently advanced, the plate is held under the water until all trace of the developing solution has been washed away, which may be known by the plate assuming a smooth, glossy appearance, but while any trace of the developer remains on the surface, it will have a streaked or mottled appearance, as if oil had been poured on—some such appearance as it presents when too soon withdrawn from the nitrate bath.

During the development of the plate, if one part comes up quicker, or if there is more than one picture, and the time of exposure has been difficult and one picture develops quicker than the other, the action of the developer may be checked on that one by holding it under running water, allowing the water to touch only the particular part where the effect is to be produced. By holding that portion of the plate lower than the other, the development may still go on, on the remaining portion of the plate, and the pictures may thus be made alike in tone and brilliancy.

The plate having been developed and washed, is now to be fixed or cleared, for which purpose it is placed in a bath of a solution of cyanide of potassium. This bath, for reasons given elsewhere, should be kept in an upright bath-dish, inclosed in a box having a close fitting cover. The solution should be sufficiently strong to dissolve the remaining iodide of silver from the surface of the plate in from three to five seconds, when the plate should be taken out and again subjected to a still more careful washing, in order that every trace of cyanide of potassium be removed from the plate. If the picture had, by over-exposure in the camera or over-development, been made too light, it may be improved by allowing it to remain for a longer time in the fixing solution; or it may be dipped in the cyanide and held over the flame of a lamp or gas-burner, that the heat may accelerate the action of the cyanide on the Collodion film, or on the silver of which the image is composed.

The action of the cyanide is, first, to dissolve the iodide of silver, after which it will attack the metallic silver of the image, and by reducing the deposit of silver in the high lights and elsewhere on the plate, it has the effect of darkening the image; or, by thinning the deposit of silver, what remains is less opaque, thus allowing the black surface of the plate to show through the shadows and half-tones.

The plate having been perfectly washed, is now taken to the light and submitted to the inspection of the lady and her friends, if she is accompanied by any. If it proves satisfactory, it may be finished at once; or if not quite pleasing to the sitter, it may be placed in a rack and another plate prepared and exposed in the same manner as before, introducing such changes as the sitter may suggest as desirable, always taking care to ascertain the exact nature of the change required, unless it is quite apparent to yourself from the defects of the picture already made. In such case, it becomes the duty of the operator—to himself as well as the lady—to make another sitting, suggesting and making such alterations as may appear desirable.

A satisfactory picture having been secured, it should be thoroughly washed, taken to the drying stove, and the water evaporated from its surface by heat. All Ferrotypes are, or should be, colored or tinted, which is done by applying finely pulverized *dry* colors to the pictures with a soft camels hair pencil brush. Ordinarily only the cheeks and lips are tinted, which takes but a few moments as the color is applied quickly, the brush being pressed more closely to the parts where the color is to be strongest. The surplus color is then brushed off with a soft blender, which also blends the color on the cheeks from the highest softly down to those parts requiring none at all. After the coloring the pictures are varnished, and again subjected to heat, unless the varnish is of a self-drying nature. Most Ferrotype varnishes require a gentle heat to produce the glossy finish so necessary to the surface.* The varnish having become perfectly dry, the picture is trimmed; that is, the edges are cut, reducing the plate to the proper size, and fitting it for the envelope case, or frame in which it may be placed. This operation, as well as all others described, requires to be done neatly. If the picture is to be put in an envelope, the edges should be cut perfectly straight, the corners neatly clipped, and, as far as possible, a finished appearance given to the work, remembering that "anything that is worth doing at all, is worth doing well;" which is a good motto for the Ferrotypist, who should always strive to improve the quality of his work. In many cases it takes no more time to do a thing in a first-class manner than to do it in a careless and slovenly way; it may only require the thought and ambition to excel. Trifles make up the sum of perfection, as was justly remarked by the celebrated sculptor who,

---

* There have been a large number of varnishes prepared and sold for the purpose of protecting the surface of ferrotypes, but none of them have sustained the reputation that is accorded to Anthony's Diamond Varnish. It possesses high gloss, is almost entirely colorless, and does not turn yellow as most others do.

Those, however, who prefer a spirit varnish may be as well pleased with Anthony's Flint or the Mountfort Varnish, both of which are quite good for the purpose.

having showed a piece of work to a friend, afterward spent six months hard labor on it. When the friend came again he admired the wonderful perfection of the statue, but could not imagine when or how the artist had bestowed so much labor on it until it was explained.

The Ferrotypist being compelled, by the nature of his business, to work rapidly should work deliberately; that is, with thought, putting brains in his work. A quick stroke may be an efficient one; a slow stroke may be very carelessly and aimlessly delivered. The difference is that the former is, as it were, delivered by brain force, the latter mechanically.

The Collodion process, to be worked successfully, requires thought, care, and skill, and it should be the aim of every intelligent Ferrotypist to improve his work, not being satisfied even with better than he has ever heretofore done; but let his aim be onward and upward, and his motto Excelsior.

CHAPTER X.

FOG, AND OTHER CAUSES OF FAILURE.

The practice of photography, in any of its branches, is beset by almost innumerable difficulties, especially to the student. Many of these difficulties are merely the result of his slight acquaintance with the properties of the substances which he employs, and of their combinations. His knowledge of those substances, however, will rapidly increase, and with the increase of knowledge, the recurrence of fogs and other technical errors and causes of failure will be less and less frequent, until, perhaps, they cease altogether.

It is expected that those who adopt the methods and processes recommended in the foregoing pages, and exercise a conscientious care in all the various operations, as directed in the article on the Collodion process, will be comparatively free from failures of any kind, even from the first; yet still, as these disturbances sometimes trouble even the most experienced, it is hoped that the few concise directions given hereafter, as to the mode of procedure in such cases, will enable the operator to overcome all such difficulties and their causes. Careful and observing operators very rarely "get into a fog;"

they are of the class of men, who, when "things do not work well," begin to look intelligently for the cause, and in most instances do not fail to find it.

We have in the Collodion process a very important trio of essential parts—the nitrate bath, the Collodion, and the developer; these three must strictly harmonize to produce good results. The silver solution must be of a suitable strength for the Collodion, as the Collodion must be salted or excited to accommodate the number of grains of silver to the fluid ounce of the silver solution, and the developer must so harmonize with the sensitized plate, as to flow evenly and smoothly over the surface; in fact, to amalgamate with the surface during that process. To do this, it must not have too much alcohol for a new bath, or too little for an old one. Again, this trio is so intimately and closely related, that a watchful care must always be kept to maintain the proper balance of its parts. If the proper strength of the nitrate bath is 45 grains to the fluid ounce, we should hardly expect good results from a 25 grain solution with the same Collodion. Care must be bestowed in keeping the bath at its proper strength; Collodion which has been kept for a time is likely to become decomposed, thus settling free iodine, giving it a deep reddish color; accompanying this, is a loss of ether by evaporation; these things must be attended to according to directions in article on Collodion.

We also have been taught, or know by experience, that the developing solution should have certain fixed proportions of iron, acid, and alcohol, to produce certain effects. What folly to expect as good results from greater or less proportions! and thus, as I have said before, a more intimate knowledge of the properties of the nitrate of silver, of the qualities of salted or excited Collodion, and of the developing effects of iron, will soon do away with many of the difficulties and causes of failure under which the photographer labored at an earlier day.

Theoretically, we should use for our silver and other solutions ingredients which are chemically pure; but, practically, this is not the case, as we very rarely use water which is chemically pure—even distilled water is not so. Our nitrate of silver, in a great many cases, is adultered; in fact, a certain amount of adulteration is necessary to produce the beautiful whiteness and brilliancy of its crystals, before it is considered fit for the market. And so with other chemicals and solutions used in photographic studios; they are all more or less impure. To this adulteration or impurity, then, as well as to inharmonious action of the various solutions, may be attributed many of the technical errors of our processes, and, in fact, from these fruitful sources arise many of the failures incidental to the practice of the Collodion process.

What we call "Fog," is a general obscuration over the whole plate; it may arise from the silver bath, from the Collodion, or from diffused light in the camera-box, the plate-holder, or the dark-room.

A silver bath, newly prepared, will in many cases produce pictures entirely or partially obscured by fog, in which case the fog is occasioned by organic matter held in suspension in the bath, which, being deposited on the plate during the process of coating with iodide, on exposure turns black, because it is more sensitive to the light than the pure iodide of silver. To correct the tendency to fog on the part of a new bath, add a few drops of chemically pure nitric acid, the effect of which will be to change the organic matter from a state of suspension (which is that of floating in and through the solution in innumerable fine atoms) to a state of solution, which is to be dissolved in the same manner as the nitrate of silver is dissolved by water. With a new bath, fog sometimes proceeds from an insufficient supply of iodide of potassium, of which every new bath should have nearly if not quite as much as it will take up. (See directions for exciting the bath in article on silver.) Sometimes old Collodion will work well with a new bath, when a sample of new will not work at all.

When the end or side of a plate is fogged, it probably comes from the holder; the remedy is to dry and varnish the holder with naphtha varnish.

Fogs from the admission of light into the camera box, the holder, or the dark room, are not the same in appearance as fog from the bath, being of a lighter color, and being apparently in the substance of the film, while that from the bath appears to lie upon the surface, and can frequently be removed with a piece of cotton or a soft brush.

Fogs are caused sometimes by the developer, more often in hot weather than otherwise, and by foreign substances getting into the developer.

To ascertain the cause of fog, first see that your camera-box and plate-holder are tight, and that the dark room admits no light; then change your developer, cleaning the bottle carefully, and if the weather is hot, cool the developer; next test the bath, and if neutral, add a drop or two of acid. On trying a plate, you will probably find that the fog has disappeared.

Transparent spots, or as they appear on the ferro-plate, black spots, are produced by particles of dust adhering to the surface of the plate. Very often, brushing the plate to remove dust from the surface, produces an electrical condition, which causes it to attract and hold small particles of varnish, which chip off the edges, and particles of dust also adhere to the lip of the Collodion bottle, and upon coating the plate they become incorporated with the film, and produce black spots on the plate when developed. When these occur, the remedy suggests itself: clean the Collodion bottle, and remove all the dust from the shelves where the plates stand.

Comets are particles of dust which fall upon the surface of a coated plate, or are received from the bath, on the plate being dipped. These spots of dust or dirt adhere to the surface of the Collodion, and when the developing solution is applied, they form nuclei for heavier deposits of silver, little tails of silver forming in the direction of the flow. Remedy: filter the bath, and keep always covered, and keep the dark room free from dust.

The silver bath receives from each plate that is immersed a portion of its iodide. After the bath becomes saturated, and can take up no more, this iodide forms itself into innumerable particles or crystals of iodo-nitrate of silver, commonly called "free iodide." This free iodide deposits itself on the surface of the plate, producing (on the negative) what is called "pinholes," and in the ferrotype the whole surface is covered with tiny black spots. For remedy, see article on silver. If not convenient to change the bath at once, reverse the dipper and turn the Collodion surface of the plate downward.

Perpendicular streaks are caused most generally by the bath being either too strong or too weak for the Collodion. An old and slightly decomposed Collodion causes streaks. Streaks will show themselves on plates which have been dipped before the Collodion has properly set, and also on plates which have not been perfectly coated with iodide of silver.

Horizontal lines are caused by the stoppage of the motion of the plate when first dipped; it is sometimes advantageous to immerse a plate very slowly, but the motion should not cease until the plate is submerged, as every stoppage will make a fine line parallel with the surface of the solution.

Crapy appearance of the film always proceeds from a watery Collodion—oblique lines, in the direction of the return of the surplus from the plate, very frequently show themselves when such a Collodion is used. Coat plates very quickly with such a Collodion, and keep the plate incessantly in motion from the side to the end.

White spots are caused by excess of nitric acid. Sometimes when this acid is used to remedy a fogging bath, too much may have been added, in which case it manifests itself in white spots on the picture.

The developer should be flowed very gently upon the plate, and always on the end where the Collodion film is thickest, (the corner from whence the surplus is run off,) otherwise a bright spot or space like a fan in shape, will extend from the corner toward the center of the plate. A plate which has been exposed the usual time, and the image upon which will not develop clearly, appearing to be under-exposed, has not received a perfect coat of iodide of silver. When plates are moved about in the bath, to accelerate the coating, they sometimes present a smooth surface before they are perfectly coated. Better, where time will permit, to allow the plate to rest in the silver bath until coated.

If the Collodion film slips from the plate after development, the fault is most likely with the plate. A greasy or imperfectly cleaned surface will sometimes not hold the film. If the plates are first-class, a drop of water in the Collodion will make it hold, or it may sometimes be sufficient to breathe upon the plate just before coating with Collodion.

When the developing solution is too strong, too warm, and sometimes when there is a deficiency of acid, it will leave a scum, often called a veil, over the pictures. When the film repels the developer, add a little more alcohol to the latter.

Small white circles often appear on plates which have been imperfectly cleaned. In fact imperfectly cleaned plates are a fruitful source of defects and failure. Oily spots or lines appear on the surface of a plate that has been dipped and immediately withrawn before the ether on the surface of the plate has had time to be washed off. These lines look like a confusion of fine circles, presenting a mottled appearance. Stains often appear on the plate when the holder or slide is dirty.

In view of the many defects that arise from dust and dirt in the dark-room, in the plate-holder and in the other vessels and receptacles, it can not but strike the attention of the reader that the best way is to keep everything perfectly clean, and the camera-box and plate-holder in thorough repair and good working order. The number of "take overs" which are rendered necessary in a good many establishments, every week, by dust from the dark-room, stains, etc., from the plate-holder, and by diffused light in the camera-box, holder and dark-room, cost a great deal more than would suffice to keep these things in first-rate order and scrupulously clean.

Another source of failures and annoyance, is finger-marks on the surface of the plate. If the operator himself cuts the plates, these can only be entirely avoided by wearing gloves while so engaged. But when the plates are purchased cut to the regular sizes, there is no excuse for such marks and stains, as the plates should always be handled in the most dainty manner imaginable, by the two edges, unless when "flowing" with Collodion, or during the process of development, and then the smallest portion of the corner, only sufficient to afford a safe hold, should be taken between the thumb and finger, as stains and streaks very frequently result from contact of the developer with the thumb during development.

CHAPTER XI.

COMPOSITION AND ILLUMINATION.

Among Ferrotypists, and I might say among Photographers generally, there is less known of, and consequently less skill exhibited, in composition and illumination than in almost any other particular of the art. More and more is the attention of photographers being drawn to this subject; and justly so, for this has been the neglected ground, while other, less productive fields, have been thoroughly and almost exhaustively cultivated.

We find in photographic manuals and books of reference long chapters treating of lenses, silver baths, Collodions, etc., etc., but few give any instruction on the more important subjects of this article; and even they, in such a scientifically obscure manner as to afford very little information or assistance to the operator in posing, draping, and lighting a subject in order to produce an artistic effect.

It is certainly a good thing to know how to make gun-cotton, to understand fully the properties and qualities of ether, alcohol and the salts used for exciting Collodion; how to compound or to separate and to test for purity the various chemicals and solutions used in the photographic atelier. It is necessary that we should understand intimately the qualities of nitrate of silver, its changes under the action of light, and how to facilitate that action, and render it certain and permanent. These and a great many more of the principles of our art we may be perfectly familiar with,—thanks to the untiring diligence with which researches on those subjects have been conducted by photographic experimentalists, and to the general diffusion of such knowledge in works on chemistry and the current photographic publications, but very little is written or said about the æsthetics of photography. The one should have and has been done, but the other should not have been left undone.

Photographers generally are a wide-awake class, and know the importance and necessity of study, and they undoubtedly make good use of the advantages they possess in acquainting themselves with the exigencies of the situation; it is, therefore, reasonable to suppose that had they possessed equal advantages for the study of illumination and the pose, the artistic helps to our art, as they have had for that which relates to the more scientific portions, there would have been a sooner awakening to the fact that every effort has been put forth seemingly with a view to make photography equivalent to an exact science; that is, a photography of arbitrary rules and laws, rather than a photography of artistic taste and judgment. It would appear that the great object has been to make processes certain in their results rather than to make the results beautiful or artistic.

Photography has been spoken of in terms of contempt, and the dilettantis of art have turned away with scorn from the contemplation of meritorious photographic productions, because, they said, there was too much of the severe and too close attention to minor details. No attempt having been made to concentrate the interest and to draw the eye to some central point of beauty; they profess to find no gratification in the contemplation of the "naked truth," as the Sun picture has been called by one of this fastidious class.

The time has now arrived when the demand for something more than a mere likeness has brought into the field some who have "taken up arms to conquer;" and from the wonderful progress already made, it will not be strange if, in a short time Photograph and indeed Ferrotype portraits and miniatures will be produced which shall, in every point of excellence, rival the best productions of the pencil and brush. Indeed, an evident effort is being put forth to learn how to veil the nakedness, to smooth the roughness, and to soften the asperities of which we have so long been uncomplaining, if not satisfied witnesses. It is beginning to dawn on the minds of the average photographic artist that the sun, all this time, has been merely doing that which untaught minds and hands had prepared for him to do. He had seized on, at our bidding, all the prominence and all that obtruded itself upon the first sight, and had very faithfully portrayed it on our silver mirror. But at last some have awakened to the fact that our all-able and all-willing artist is quite as well pleased, and as capable, to do the bidding of a Solomon as he is that of the meanest itinerant picture maker in the country—quite as willing to heighten artistically the beauty of a Scott-Siddons as to exaggerate the ugliness of a Caliban—to hide in shadows the disagreeable, and to smooth down the projections and wrinkles, as he had been to force them with relentless exaggeration upon our attention.

There is, then, an awakening to the fact that instead of placing our patron bolt upright in a seat, with his elbow on a table, his arm forming an angle of a square, his face to the front, showing one corner of his mouth turned up and the other down, giving the appearance of a round white spot, with two holes for eyes,[*] and a diagonal or oblique slit across it for a mouth. It would answer the aims of portraiture as well to place him at his ease on a handsome chair, reclining slightly for greater comfort, the good side of his face turned to view, a little light to fall in

---

[*] See Mr. Whipple's article on "Educate the People," in the "Photographic World" for August, 1872.

front to soften the lines, a graded back-ground to give atmospheric effect, and the direct light reduced to give roundness and solidity, so that the result might have some claim to be called artistic.

Photography is a truth-teller, with or without qualification, and it is said that the truth should not always be told; such being the case, we should call our artistic qualities into play in posing and lighting our sitter, and in the arrangement of draperies and accessories.

When our long, gaunt, six-foot customer comes in, and demands his picture taken standing, (full length portraits are so popular with that class,) we mildly—or otherwise—remonstrate. We tell him that our artistic taste will be outraged by taking his picture at his worst, instead of at his best. We also tell him, when he expresses a preference for a front view of his face, that any other is equally a likeness; that his is probably seen as many times in profile, or three-quarters, as in front, and we try to hint that the front view of his face is not the most prepossessing, and if he has any pleasing point of view of his face, we would much rather look at it than that his full and unmitigated ugliness should obtrude itself upon our vision. We strive, by the aid of posing, drapery, and lighting, to give character to the sitter, and individuality to our work. In all this, art comes to our assistance and relief, and we are successful as far as we understand the application of art principles. In the subsequent manipulations we apply our scientific knowledge, and it is in this latter, rather than in the former, that we have made the greatest progress. Art, then, as applied to photography, is the effort to disguise the "naked truth," and to change the dictum of the celebrated painter that "photography was justice without mercy," making it, rather, "justice tempered by mercy."

Photography, takes the human form, sitting bolt upright, without an effort to soften or improve. Art comes in, and, behold! the pose is changed from rigidity to ease; the light is tempered and made to fall with softening effect upon the features; draperies are employed to give depth of shadow and brilliancy of effect, and the resulting portrait, instead of being barely tolerable—because of likeness to the original—is praised and valued highly, and secures for the skillful operator the gratitude as well as the patronage of all concerned.

It is a difficult thing to form a system of rules and regulations for the guidance of the uninitiated in the application of the principles of art to photography; a thing which I am not aware of having been attempted yet, nor shall I attempt it in this connection, but I shall endeavor to give some hints which the reader may find of advantage or not, as he may choose to follow them up, or apply them in his daily practice. Under the head of Composition, we would include posing, draperies, and the arrangement of accessories.

When called upon to pose the patrons of our establishment, we should first inquire of each individual their especial preference as to position and view. If they have none, then it becomes our duty to suggest; and to do this intelligently, we should first scan the face, figure, and style of dress of the subject, making up our minds as quickly as possible as to which would be best. To do this, we must consider with reference to a standing position; is he or she tall or short, or of medium height, of light or heavy frame, of smooth or wrinkled face, and with regard to style of dress, whether it is new and handsomely fitting or otherwise.

The greatest difficulty will be experienced in giving an agreeable and graceful effect to a standing male figure. The attempt should never be made without protest, except under the most favorable circumstances, which are, first, medium height, good figure, well-fitting clothes; second, suitable accessories to fill the pictures; third, ability on the part of the artist to so pose and arrange, so as to take away from the sitter the conscious look as of having a picture taken, almost inseparable from the position.

With the female standing figure, there is much less difficulty; the lines of the dress tend to support each other, and the drapery, gracefully flowing, removes any appearance of stiffness incidental to the position. For standing positions of both males and females, some suitable support to lean against or on, is a wonderful relief from the worst difficulties of the position. Attention must, however, be given to the proper balance of the figure; the center of gravity must be maintained to the eye, or the effect would be distressing.

Tall persons of either sex should never be photographed in standing positions, unless three-quarter or half-length views are taken. They are also very difficult subjects in sitting positions, when the whole figure is taken; these can be more satisfactorily treated in bust pictures or half-lengths, sitting.

Short, fleshy persons should have bust pictures or vignettes.

Very frequently, however, the most unsuitable positions are chosen. In such cases, the chief reliance (for producing a good effect), must be placed in position and drapery, with suitable accessories; no general rules can be given suitable to all cases, except those of balance and contrast.

In posing the figure, and in the arrangement of the accessories, perpendicular and horizontal parallel lines must be avoided as much as possible; the lines of the figure and accessories should converge to a point in a pyramidal form, or in an oblique direction from below upward and outward, with lines of support, etc.; as, for instance, a soldier might rest upon his rifle or sword, a gentleman might balance himself with his walking-stick. So important is the balance of the figure, that it must not be neglected in any style of picture, being equally necessary in the vignette as in the full length.

When full length pictures are made, the camera should be elevated to about two-thirds the height of the subject; the same for half-length, standing. For sitting pictures, the lens should be about as high as the chin of the sitter. The arrangement of the drapery should always be carefully studied; curtains, table-covers, etc., can be used with very good effect in creating pictorial effect. A piece of dark drapery can be made a contrast to some light portion of dress; a handsome silk curtain or velvet table-cover thrown over the back of the posing-chair, falling in graceful folds to the floor, affords a fine relief to the sometimes stiff lines of a lady's dress, or to the perpendicular lines of the male standing figure; a fold of drapery can be used to good effect to cover or hide from view the foot of the head-rest. For figures leaning on the arm or over the back of the posing-chair, the effect is much improved by throwing the drapery carelessly over the arm or back, as the case may be.

In making positions, to have every thing subservient to the portrait is the rule, and a heaping together of the odds and ends of the gallery to make a picture, should be avoided as a gross violation of good taste, and an imposition of the patron who wants a likeness, and not a picture of tables, chairs, flower-pots, busts, etc., etc., *ad nauseum*.

When making a position, the artist should avoid touching the clothes or person of the subject as much as possible. The Ferrotypist can scarcely keep his hands and person as neat and clean as the professional positionist in a first-class gallery. He should, therefore, recollect that in many instances his fingers leave a stain wherever they touch, no matter how clean they may look; besides, the hands are almost always wet or damp. To take, then, the head of a lady between the palms of the hands, as I have seen done, is an outrage. The best way is to stand some little distance off, and scanning the position, give the subject verbal directions for any desired change of position. In case you can not make yourself understood or obeyed, then, by taking the head between the tips of the fingers, touching the hair, and avoiding to touch the face, the head may very gently be turned as desired. In most cases, by touching one hand to the side or back of the head, will be sufficient to apply what force is necessary to make the change. The Ferrotypist should learn to make positions quickly. The assistant should have the plate sensitized while the position is being made.

A kind and obliging treatment of customers is the best way to secure a good expression; at the same time, that nothing of an offensive nature should be allowed any-where in sight, such as a dirty spittoon, a broken piece of furniture, or a dusty chair. One of the best artist photographers in the country, on taking possession of an entirely new gallery, which was fitted up in a gorgeous manner, regardless of expense—glass-room carpeted with fine body Brussels; walls and ceiling frescoed in most beautiful and expensive manner; light of heavy plate glass, in strips of ten feet long, by two or more wide—ventured the remark that he was "going for expression" in his new gallery. In this case every thing was so well calculated to please and delight, that the remark was justified. Much may be done by an attentive operator to secure good expressions, even among poor surroundings.

It has been almost universally the rule, heretofore, and is now to a great extent, to expose the sitter to a flood of light from above, from the side, and the front—light every-where; the consequence of which has been, pictures without half tones, without modeling, and without strength or brilliancy; the lights were all high lights, the shadows all opaque. The principal cause of this tendency, has been the desire to secure rapidity of action, making short the exposure of the sensitized plate, and proceeds from an error in the expectation. Let the light be reduced; let at least two-thirds of the light be shaded, and the remainder illuminate the sitter more directly, and it will be found quite sufficient to produce properly effective high lights. In reducing or shading the greater portion of the light, it is not expected that the light will be cut off entirely, but that shades of a semi-transparent character shall be used to diminish the amount and intensity, and by diminishing to change its character from direct to diffused. Thus, an illumination of a sitter by diffused light lends a softness and roundness to the figure that contrasts beautifully with the effect of the few direct rays in producing brilliancy of the high lights, and transparency of the shadows, and what we lose in time of exposure, we more than gain in artistic excellence. A properly constructed photographic light should be of northern exposure, top and side lights combined, the side light reaching from the floor to the lower end of the top light, which should be at least ten feet from the floor, the top sash having sufficient pitch to shed the rain-water freely, so as not to leak. With such a light, properly shaded, a great variety of beautiful effects can be produced. To make this more intelligible, let us consider the side and top light separately and combined.

The light from above, when alone used, gives a flat, but soft and smooth picture, with heavy shadows under projecting parts; it is a great eradicator of wrinkles and freckles, and is as effectual in removing tan and sunburn from the complexion of the picture, as the sun is in producing it in the original. The top light also gives very good definition in the drapery, and where circumstances deprive of the advantages of a side light to be used in connection with it, very good and satisfactory work can be produced by the aid of reflectors, etc.

The side light, when used alone, is a dreadful destroyer of complexions. If a freckle has hidden so far under the skin as not to be visible or scarcely so, to the naked eye, the side light drags the hidden thing to light, and exposes it in much exaggerated ugliness to the horrified gaze. In like manner, it by giving a brighter high light increases the density of the shadows by contrast. While the top light gives a flat smooth picture, the side light lends strength, coarseness and rotundity; while the top light smooths over the imperfections of complexion, the side light magnifies and increases them; and, finally, while the top light gives good definition of drapery, the side light makes dark drapery a black mass, black hair blacker still, and is altogether a difficult light to manage alone, (that is, without a top light,) even with the best appliances; but with the top and side light together, and with a northern exposure, we have the *"par excellence"* of lights. The top light serves to neutralize the bad qualities of the side light, and *vice versa*.

Thus, our customer has a smooth face, small features, and a black coat. Taken under the top light, we get a face without character, hair all white on the top, and a coat that would appear to have been very glossy at least. We will remove the subject to the combined top and side lights, and we have a decided change. By shading the top light, so as to illuminate mostly from the side, we give character to a rather insipid face, at the same time that we have sufficient light from above to soften and relieve the shadows. The hair, too, which before was all too white on the upper portion of the head, we can now view of the exact shade we desire; and the coat that was all gray, we now have as black as can be desired, consistent with good definition. Thus we see, that when we want greater strength and contrast, we have only to use more light from the side than from the top; and when we want to take the picture of a blonde with golden hair, we sit her well out under the top light and shade the side quite close. Thus we correct the faults of one light by the good qualities of the other.

It will be very apparent, that a knowledge of the properties of the top and side lights separately, will be of great advantage to the Ferrotypist in properly handling them when combined. For such information see the article on "Glassroom." In this connection the principal object is to show what can be done by the use of these two lights to overcome the defects of nature, and to give character to our work.

As an instance of what may be done, let us take, for example, a lady or gentleman whose face is freckled. These freckles are very unsightly in the Ferrotype, and we can not remove them by any operation outside of the process by which they are made, as the photographer does when he "retouches" his negative, a process by which alabaster complexions can and pretty generally are given to all indiscriminately. They may well exclaim, Great is the negative, but the pencil is its *profit!*

The Ferrotypist must "come the artful" over such cases; and although he may not remove or hide them altogether, he can do wonders with no other agency than light. For that purpose we will shade all of the side light, if the day is clear, allowing just enough to relieve the shadows under the nose and chin. We will shade half of the top light, thus securing a larger portion of diffused light to help to relieve the shadows and to soften the whole. The direct light comes from above, producing a high light on the top of the forehead and on the nose, and passing smoothly over the face, lights up all parts with an even illumination, the result of which in the picture will be to greatly improve the complexion and please the patron.

The next person who requires our service is an old gentleman whose face is much wrinkled. That his portrait must please him it must not exaggerate these lines of age, but rather smooth them out if we may. How shall we proceed? If we illuminate him by side light alone, we shall make every perpendicular line a furrow, if by top light, we shall produce the same effect with the horizontal lines. We should, indeed, give him "the furrowed brow, the wrinkled front of age," with a vengeance. Rather let us move the background and seat the gentleman facing the light, directly or nearly so; the light will now tend to render less prominent the signs of age, by lighting equally the depressions and the projections. Some skill will be required to relieve the eye, but a little thought will not fail to suggest the proper means.

As a general rule, it is proper to take front views of all persons who are "hollow-cheeked," or have long faces, and three-quarter views or profiles for those who have round full moon faces, or who are very fleshy. There are many exceptions to such a rule as the above, as for example, a long faced person whose cheeks are not sunken, a three-quarter view may give a very handsome oval, and frequently round faced fleshy persons will not bear a three-quarter or profile view.

By a course of studying the faces that come before the operator, he will acquire the ability to decide almost immediately, on viewing the subject, as to the best and most favorable pose of the figure, and view of the face. This is the only means whereby such a knowledge can be acquired, as there is no possibility of forming a system of posing suited to all figures and faces. Common sense will suggest to the operator to make the most of the good points, and to hide or subdue, as much as possible, the bad ones. If the subject has a fine figure, place in such a position as to show it to advantage.

In the composition of a group place those who are good looking in the most conspicuous position, or where they will be in the line of the focus; the ill-favored ones will always be best suited if placed in less conspicuous positions out of the line of sharpest focus. Great attention should be given in the formation of a group to preserve a just balance of all the parts, both as regards the size and height, as well as color and dress. The tall members of the party, if they are to stand, should be placed in the rear center; if they are to sit, they should be placed on the ends. Those of dark complexion and dress should be placed nearest the light. I have known a finely posed group spoiled by a black dress being placed farthest from the light, so that when all the rest developed beautifully, the black dress was a dense mass of shadow. In the composition of a picture, where there is but one figure, with certain accessories suggestive of action, either in-doors or without, attention must be given not to overload the picture with a great quantity of furniture of fanciful articles, nor to dispose those which are used in such a manner as to offend the sense of the laws of gravity, the artistic, or the beautiful. If the view is of an outside character, attention must be given to those parts requiring more prominence than others, that they be placed so as to receive it, and that the character of the illumination shall not altogether belie the effect of the picture; or, in other words, that the illumination may be from the same general direction for the ground and subject, and not, as were the celebrated or rather notorious "spirit photographs," made at one time in New York, by a man named Mumler, the lighting of his sitter being in one direction, and illumination of the picture of the "spirit" (supposed to be of some relation,) from a contrary direction, producing a very incongruous effect indeed, and giving rise to astonishment in the mind that people should be found so grossly credulous as to be imposed upon by such trickery.

CHAPTER XII.

VIGNETTES, MEDALLIONS, ETC.

VIGNETTES are a very popular style of picture, and every gallery should be prepared to make them. They were formerly made by taking a piece of glass, of the size of the plate on which the Vignette is to be made, and holding it over a candle flame, so as to blacken an oval shaped Vignette in the center of the glass. Having exposed the plate in the camera, return to the dark-room, take the plate from the holder, place the vignette glass over the sensitive surface, bringing the opaque part as nearly over the head and shoulders as possible; then open the door and expose for a few seconds to the light. Withdraw and develop, when the light will be found to have whitened all that part of the picture not covered by the opaque part of the glass, thus producing a Vignette by a very tedious process applicable only to one at a time. The next process was a patented one and required to be done in the camera, by having an extra slide of glass, with an opaque center, to cover the head and shoulders as before. The exposure having been made, the tube was covered and the glass slide pushed in, when the tube was uncovered; and after a few seconds the slide is replaced, the holder withdrawn to the dark chamber, and the plate developed. This process offered a little more certainty than the former, but was never generally adopted, although applicable to the negative as well as to the positive picture.

The plan generally adopted, and that which is in use in all the best Ferrotype galleries, is to cut an oval or other suitable shaped opening in the center of a sheet of white card-board, the edge of the opening to be serrated or toothed, so as to cause the ground to blend softly with the portions of the figure and drapery. The card-board is commonly placed on a frame (made and sold by stock dealers for that purpose), and being placed between the sitter and the camera, at a sufficient distance from the camera to cause the proper softening of the outline, the exposure is made as usual, and upon development the card-board will be found to have blended beautifully with the white back-ground, softening the edges where it covers the clothing and drapery of the sitter.

This process has the further recommendation that many sittings may be made consecutively, and all will be equally good at the same time. The Vignetter may be adjusted to produce the best possible effects, as it shows plainly on the object-glass of the camera. When at the proper distance from the camera, and when showing the proper portion of the shoulders, changes may be rapidly made to show more or less of the figure by an adjustable stand, so that all varieties can be produced with the greatest facility.

The usual method of adjustment is to stand with the vignette in the hand, having placed it at what you consider the proper place, and look over the edge of the opening into the camera so as not to obstruct the reflection of the sitter. One will easily see from that position if the Vignette is too high or too low, or if too much to the right or left; by moving it nearer to the camera the opening is enlarged, showing more of the figure, while by placing it nearer to the sitter the blending becomes more abrupt and the opening smaller, embracing the shoulders closely. Vignettes can also be made two or three in a group, by having the opening sufficiently large or by placing it nearer the camera. There are a variety of useful openings, among which are the round, egg-shape, and half circle. All of these are to be used with white grounds. They can, however, be used with gray grounds, sometimes with very good effect.

To make Vignettes by this apparatus, it should be the endeavor of the operator to have the same amount of intensity of light on the Vignette as on the back-ground, in order that they may be of the same shade or tone in the finished picture. This is easily done by turning the Vignette toward the light, either top or side, although it is generally better to turn it toward the top light.

Vignettes with gray and dark grounds may be produced by the same process, using a dark background, of course, instead of the white; and to have the Vignette of the same shade as the ground, turn it from the light. By looking in the camera you can easily see when you have it dark enough. Having arranged the Vignette to satisfaction, proceed as before.

The best form of stand for the Vignette was invented by Mr. I. H. Stoddard, and is manufactured and sold by E. & H. T. Anthony & Co., and can be had through any stock dealer. It consists of a light wooden stand, with a hollow upright piece, similar to the stand of the headrest. The frame upon which the card-board is fastened is pivoted within another frame, which is set on a piston, moving in the hollow upright of the stand, so fitted as to remain in any position without dropping. These stands are not patented; or if they are, the usual liberality of the Messrs. Anthony is shown by the low price at which they are sold.

THE MEDALLION FERROTYPE.

The Medallion Ferrotype is another instance of the variety of beautiful effects possible to be produced in these pleasing pictures, the finished and handsome effect produced is very attractive, and recommends the picture at once to the attention of the observer. When made with care, the Medallion Ferrotype is quite equal in effect to the photograph of the same name, and can be produced with much more ease.*

I believe it has not been more than two years since this popular style was introduced in photography, and at the present day there is not, probably, a photographer in the country who has not felt the demand for this pleasing style of portrait and made an effort to comply with it. In fact, so great has been the demand as to create a new article of use, viz., the "cut-out," thousands of which are made and sold every-where, and the printed directions accompanying them have probably been as eagerly sought after as any thing else; and as is always the case, the demand for these simple disks of paper has stimulated the ingenuity of the producers to the inevitable result: (the patented article,) so that medallion disks of metal and semi-opaque substances in conjunction, to produce serrated and Mosaic borders, which it is supposed would be a joy forever to a Sandwich Islander, and well calculated to drive an aboriginal South Australian into fits of admiration.

The Medallion Ferrotype, however, is quite another thing, it is not a patented article, neither is the apparatus by which the effect produced, and I hasten to lay the whole process before the

---

* See sample of medallion Ferrotype accompanying this work.

universal American public, before that devoutly to be detested consummation takes place.

The apparatus required, then, is the small revolving or the conical back-ground, but as both of those articles are patented (!), let us have a light frame of pine wood, upon which we will stretch a cloth ground not more than four feet square; but I suppose that three feet square might be large enough. Now, if it is desirable to produce the effect of the revolving or of the conical grounds, let us shade one-half of the ground by passing something between it and the side light, so as to make the part of the ground nearest the light a shade darker than the rest. This can very easily be done by placing a shade between the ground and the light, advancing it far enough to throw the shadow where it is wanted. We now cause the sitter to assume the desired position, adjust the drapery, and arrange the light so as to produce the desired effect; having done which, we place in front of the individual (whose portrait we are about to cause the sun to take for us) another frame, which supports a large sheet of white card-board, which is cut an oval opening, sufficiently large to allow the head and shoulders to be exposed, when the frame is placed immediately over them, so as to be in the same focus as the face of the person sitting. We have now, to produce the desired effect, a white border, with a sharp cut edge around the head and shoulders, behind which, throwing it into relief, is the darker ground.

This latter frame must be supported by braces, at an angle which will allow the light from above to illuminate the whole surface. By means of these braces, we can regulate the amount of light desired to produce the proper effect. This apparatus may be made of the lightest materials, and every artist should be able to make the frames for himself. If white cardboard may not be procurable, any other color can be pasted over with white paper, and, if neatly done, will answer the purpose equally as well. Great care should be exercised in cutting the oval opening to have the edges clean cut, and the oval not too short or too long. Having procured your frame, suspend the card-board or medallion opening, with light cords running over the top of the frame, and attached to weights sufficient to balance it, so that in adjusting it over the sitter it may be raised or lowered at pleasure, always remaining where placed. When not in use, the whole may be placed conveniently aside, so as not to be in the way, yet still ready to hand. The ability to do the largest amount of *good* work in the shortest time, so as not to offend the patron of your gallery by any appearance of undue haste, nor, in case you are crowded, to waste valuable time by running here and there for that which should be at hand, is sedulously to be cultivated.

Another and, in many cases, very pleasing style of medallion, is made by using a white ground, and having in the back of the camera a suitable oval opening, which would give the head and shoulders, relieved by a properly shaded ground, surrounded by a clean black oval. Sometimes very beautiful effects are produced by this means. Ornamental borders are easily produced by cutting the edges of the opening in the back of the camera, or in perforating it with fanciful patterns sufficiently large to allow the light to pass. To produce the best effect in this way, the plate should lie as close as possible to the opening, in order to get sharpness of outline.

THE NON-REVERSED

FERROTYPE,

— A —

POSITIVE PHOTOGRAPHIC IMPRESSION

ON ADAMANTEAN FERRO PLATES,

WITH A FULL DESCRIPTION OF THE APPARATUS AND
PROCESS OF PRODUCTION, ACCOMPANIED BY

A Specimen Picture.

— BY —

E. M. ESTABROOKE,

AUTHOR OF

"The Ferrotype, and How to Make it."

1882.

Entered according to Act of Congress in the year 1868, by
JOHN DEAN & CO.,
In the Office of the Librarian of Congress, at Washington, D. C.

AUTHOR'S PREFACE.

Each copy of the previous edition of this book contained two illustrative examples of a new style of picture called the "Non-reversed Ferrotype," which were so decidedly superior to any ordinary Ferrotype as at once to attract a great deal of attention, and to cause many to inquire why the method of their production was not given.

The answer to all such inquiries, was that the pictures were made only by the Author of this book, and were the result of much study and very expensive research and experiment, and a description of their production was not particularly called for by the prospectus or title of the book.

The demand for information as to the method by which these pictures were produced very soon became so great that the publishers were induced to make a special arrangement with the writer to obtain the desired information, that it might be published in this, the second edition, of "The Ferrotype and How to Make It," and which information, including an account of the invention of the apparatus, a description of the same, and all the details incident to the successful production of Non-reversed Ferrotypes, is herewith given.

The accompanying picture is intended to be an example of what these formula and manipulations will produce when skillfully worked—and they are given as examples of fine chemical effect, perfect focus, and graceful positions—consequently it is expected that they will stimulate to renewed efforts every Ferrotypist into whose hands this book may come, to equal, if not to excel them.

To this end, a careful study of the book is recommended, and also, as far as possible, the adoption of the formula and manipulation, as well as the materials with which these pictures are made.

Messrs. E. & H. T. Anthony & Co. prepare a collodion which has no equal. This may generally be procured through any of the local dealers in photographic materials, or, if not, of the manufacturers themselves. The plates used are the celebrated Adamantean Plate, made by John Dean & Co., which I have always found uniformly excellent, and I again cordially indorse the testimony of leading Ferrotypists to their superior qualities. If these directions are followed, I am confident you can scarcely fail to achieve complete success.

NON-REVERSED FERROTYPES.

In the year 1866, being then in business at 805 Broadway, N. Y., (in a building which has since been removed to give place to one of the lofty iron structures of the day,) I conceived the idea of making pictures by the positive Collodion process, which should not have the defect of all such pictures heretofore made, either by the Daguerreotype or by the Collodion processes, viz., that of being laterally transposed—it being an admitted fact that the greatest defect of all positive pictures made directly in the camera, consisted in this very transposition of the figure in the same manner as the reflection of the form or face in a mirror, which, as every body knows, makes the right side to appear as the left, and *vice versa*, giving the parting of the hair on the wrong side, etc., etc. In considering as to the best method of overcoming this defect, it occurred to me that there was but one way in which it could be done, viz., by reflection. A suitable reflector must be placed in front of the lens, and, in practice, pictures must be made from the image of the object, and not from the object itself, for this reason. As the picture of the sitter, as now taken, is transposed in the camera, this transposition can only be overcome by transposing again; and as we can not effect two transpositions within the camera, we must effect one between the sitter and the camera lens. This can only be done by means of a reflector. At this time I commenced to experiment with various reflectors. I remembered to have heard or read a description of an apparatus that had been used during the earlier days of Daguerreotypes, by which this effect was produced, but with what degree of success I never could learn; but reasoning from the fact that I had never seen one used, and that I had never heard of such instruments being offered for sale, I concluded that it could not have been of a practical nature. However, I began to make inquiries among the stock dealers about such an instrument, and, after considerable trouble and persistence, I did find one which had been laid away upon the shelves of the old firm of Daguerreotype stock dealers—Holmes, Booth & Haydens. This instrument had passed from the memory of every body in the store but one, and by him it was considered of so little value that he very freely gave it to me without compensation. This instrument consisted of a triangular brass case, one of the faces of the right angle of which was uncovered; the other had a flange by which it could be screwed to the front of a camera lens. Having first removed the shade and cover, in the base of the triangle was fitted a square piece of plate-glass, the under or back surface of which was silvered. In use, this instrument rendered it necessary to turn the side of the camera box to the sitter, thus bringing the image of the sitter upon the glass in the reflector. I experimented with this instrument for some time, but could produce nothing which would prove satisfactory. I next tried a large cheval glass, securing the most perfect surface that I could. Upon placing the glass in front of the sitter, and pointing the camera at the reflection, I succeeded better than with the small instrument; that is, I could make the picture in slightly less time. But I was troubled in this experiment in the same manner as in the first—by double reflection—my pictures would develop with two outlines. It took me some time to get at the cause of this double outline, as I could see nothing of the kind in the object glass of my camera.

At last, placing my glass where there happened to be a stronger light reflected from its surface, I found, in a double reflection, the cause of all my troubles. The glass of the mirror and also of the small reflector being of very thick plate, it gave a reflection from both surfaces—from the front surface of the glass and from the silvered back surface. Of course, the reflection from the front or outer surface was faint, and only perceptible in the double outlines; yet, by no means at my command, could I remove or prevent it: in consequence, I was forced to give up the mirror and glass reflector. My attention was next turned to a finely-polished metallic reflecting surface, but with no better success—in consequence, I think, of the difficulty, if not the impossibility, of securing a perfectly plain surface: by which I mean a surface so perfectly even and level as to reflect all rays of light in a direction exactly parallel. It will very easily be seen that any inequality, however small, in the reflecting surface, would destroy the image: and this I found impossible to overcome: and although I had been very sanguine when I first attempted the metallic reflector, I was forced to give it up as unsuitable or unfit for the purpose.

The image reflected by one of these instruments would often be so blurred as to be undistinguishable; again, parts of the image would be perfect, but not all. This resulted, I found, from the inequalities of the metallic surface—such inequalities being produced by the tool used in burnishing the metal—and thus I was forced to the conclusion, that until a metallic surface could be ground and polished in a manner similar to that by which glass is ground and polished, the metallic reflector would not answer the purpose.

Pursuing my experiments, I procured a very fine plate of Venetian glass, and attempted to have deposited thereon a coating of metallic silver, sufficiently thick and strong to receive a high polish, without being so thick as to allow the burnishing tool to cause inequalities of the surface. In this I also failed, and for a time I gave up the idea. About this time I conceived the idea of using a prism of glass, knowing that it had the power of reflection. Upon communicating my thoughts to a friend of mine, an optician, he confirmed my impression, and offered to procure for me, from Paris, a prism of colorless glass of a suitable size for my purposes.

Eagerly accepting his offer, I gave him the dimensions of one large enough for a half-plate lens. The order was transmitted, and in due time my prism arrived from France. I had it fitted in a nice brass case, which was so arranged as to be screwed to the front of the camera tube in place of the usual shade. The brass case I caused to be lined with black velvet. With this apparatus I succeeded in producing Non-reversed pictures entirely superior to any I had heretofore made. One great drawback, however, was the length of time required for exposure. I began to cast about for means to shorten the time of exposure.

Having already the quickest working Collodion, etc., that I supposed it possible to produce, I arrived at the conclusion that I could do nothing in that direction, but must direct my efforts to make the prism more effective as a reflector. I had, I supposed, been using only its refractive power as yet. One day, as an experiment, I removed the prism from the case, and, taking out the velvet, I inserted in its place a piece of white card-board, and, to my surprise, on again trying the exposure, I found that by this simple means I was enabled to reduce the time of exposure about one-half, and got quite as perfect an image. This surprised me, as I knew that the surface of the card-board possessed a very low reflecting power, and also that its surface must be very unequal, but it seemed that the prism corrected any defect arising from such inequalities of surface.

In this way I was at once put on the right track to the long-desired object.

Taking my prism to the silver plater, I had a coating of metallic silver deposited upon its largest surface, which I caused to be covered with a strong varnish to protect it from friction, etc. I again placed it in its case, and, as may be imagined, with trembling anxiety prepared to try again its reflecting powers.

Upon coating a plate and subjecting it to an

NON-REVERSED FERROTYPES.   159

exposure of ordinary duration, I was overjoyed to find my highest hopes realized—I had secured a perfect reflector by which to produce Non-reversed positive pictures by the Collodion process.

The two cuts herewith given will convey a perfect idea of one of my methods of mounting the prism for work.

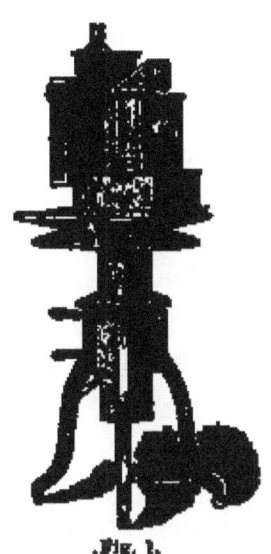 

Fig. 1.   Fig. 2.

Figure 1 shows the prism in its brass case as it rests upon the camera box. This particular reflector is of 4 inches diameter on the two faces of its right angle; the reflecting surface or back is $4 \times 5\frac{1}{4}$. It is mounted in a brass case made to screw on the front of a $\frac{1}{4}$-tube, the openings being made large enough to receive and transmit all the light the 4 inch front will admit.

Figure 2 shows the prism screwed to the tube and the cover resting on the box. This view explains the method of using the prism. The front of the prism being turned toward the sitter, presents the side of the box, and brings the ground glass and plate-holder at right angles with the sitter. The position is strange at first, but one easily becomes accustomed to it.

Another method of mounting the prism for use with the wing multiplier, is to set the tube well back in the box, and have the prism permanently fitted to an extra front, which may be slid into the front grooves of the box. By this method the lens is entirely hid from view, and a novel impression is conveyed by the appearance of the apparatus. This last method is only possible with the wing camera; the box-like front of which affords ample space for a tube as large as the box is intended for.

THE NON-REVERSED MEDALLION FERROTYPE.

This is the most beautiful of the various styles of Ferrotypes; it is also the most difficult, both because of the care required in the adjustment of the apparatus and illumination of the subject, and also because of the necessity that the positions should conform to and suit the style of the opening which produces the Medallion effect.

The cut will explain the nature of the apparatus used, and the manner of taking a Non-reversed Medallion Ferrotype, better than many words.

The apparatus consists of a light pine wood frame or support, upon which is suspended a sheet of white or gray card-board, through the center of which is cut an oval opening. The background should be dark, and, if graduated in shade, the better. The one seen in the cut is a Biglow graded revolving ground; a dark-cloth ground will answer the purpose quite well.

The background need not be more than four feet square, and may be stretched on a light frame. Through the center of the bar, which should be across the middle of the frame, a hole may be bored, by which it may be suspended on the back of the head-rest, upon the rear end of the rod which supports the head.

The medallion frame may be of light pine wood, 2 inches by 1 inch, 6 feet high, and 30 inches wide. The one in the cut is 25 inches wide; it is better to be wider.

The medallion matt may be of white cardboard, smooth or pebbled. The one in the cut is gray, and pebbled, the better to imitate the Photograph. A strip of white paper is pasted on the edge of the upper left portion of the oval, and a similar piece, but black, on the corresponding lower right.

The matt is 30x40 inches square, and glued to a light frame of $\frac{1}{2}$-inch pine; the oval opening is 16 x 22 inches.

This style of picture is much finer when made with the Rembrandt effect of light. A very beautiful effect is produced in this style of picture, after making the proper exposure, by covering the tube, and pushing the plate-holder about ¼ of an inch farther in; then remove the cover of the lens and replace it immediately. This heightens the imitation to one of the best and softest of Medallion Photographs.

The first cut explains the method of focussing the instrument; this one shows the exposure, the position of the camera, the background, reflector, etc., etc. By it also an idea may be obtained as to the method of illumination to produce the Rembrandt effect.

CONCLUSION.

As proposed in the Publisher's Preface, such improvements as have been introduced since the publication of preceding editions of THE FERROTYPE, together with a few references to matters alluded to in the course of these pages and in former editions which, in consequence of lapse of time and subsequent changes, are inaccurate, will here be given.

Most photographers must have observed the unpleasant yellowish tint which ferrotypes show on their surface. These pictures would be much more generally acceptable if the whites were produced pure. There are various modes of producing this result, but they involve a little extra trouble on the part of the operator.

One mode of avoiding this is by using a weak wash of tannin upon the plate before it is placed in the fixing bath. The solution of tannin eliminates all the sulphate of iron that may remain in the film after development and washing, and which, if left there, forms a compound with the cyanide, which gives the yellow color.

Another mode of producing fine white, and

rich, velvety black, with freedom from fog, is to proceed as follows: Make a *saturated* solution of protosulphate of iron, into which drop a solution of tannin, shaking the mixture all the while, until the precipitate of tannate of iron ceases to be redissolved; then add drop by drop of a weak solution of nitric acid until the precipitate is dissolved and the iron solution becomes of a clear bluish color. To one ounce of this add ten or eleven ounces of water, and as much acetic acid as may be found necessary. This constitutes the developer.

The patents of Wing and Southworth, alluded to in pages 42 and 43, have finally been decided invalid, and there is now no restriction in the matter of making or using cameras with sliding shields. This result was only reached after years spent in litigation, and the expenditure of thousands of dollars. In the meantime the publishers have made and improved these boxes, until they now not only excel in simplicity, but in finish and ornamental character, all others. These cameras are specifically known as the "Success" Cameras, and the large sale of them attests the correctness of the name. They combine all the recent improvements. A photographer who possesses a Success or Climax Camera Box, a Dallmeyer Portrait Lens, a Bowdish Camera Stand, and a Bowdish Chair, is provided with the most effective instruments now known to the trade.

The formula for making soluble cotton, on page 57, has never been tried by the publishers, and they therefore do not vouch for its value.

In the present edition we have omitted a few lines which were formerly to be found on page 84, regarding them more or less redundant; but the experience of photographers, from whom the proprietor of the patent endeavored to draw an income, and the excitement caused whenever he made his appearance at photographic meetings, would make an amusing episode in a photographic history. It is sufficient, however, to say, that at the present time Mr. Shaw has ceased to annoy the members of the profession by his demands. To any one in the slightest degree versed in elementary chemistry, it is surprising in the extreme that a person could be so little informed as to make the extraordinary claim that was founded on this patent.

One of the greatest improvements, so far as the æsthetic aspect of a ferrotype is concerned, has been the introduction of the tinted ferrotype plate. The appearance of a picture on one of these plates is far more agreeable than the old, ancient and unalterable black color, and ferrotypers are under great obligations in connection with them to Messrs. John Dean & Co., who are the sole manufacturers, the product being covered by a patent.

CONCLUSION. 167

Prisms, referred to on pages 157–160, are now a regular article of commerce, and made to fit any tube. They can be purchased through any of the dealers, or direct from the publishers.

As to expense, the apparatus and materials required in the making of ferrotypes have been very considerably cheapened since the earlier days, and the variety increased, according to the scale on which the business is to be conducted. For instance, the cost of lenses usually employed for the purpose is greatly reduced, and in less degree the cameras also.

THE CLIMAX CAMERA, NO. 43, FITTED WITH FOUR ¼ LENSES.

The iron plates, too, on which the pictures are made, are very much lower than formerly, and more attractive means have been devised for mounting and delivery. These particulars, however, may be all gleaned from our illustrated catalogue of photographic materials and of card stock; but for convenience, we subjoin illustrations of two of the instruments usually selected, the first being what is known as our Climax Camera No. 43, which is of excellent workmanship, and exceedingly popular on account of its comparative cheapness; the second

THE SUCCESS CAMERA O, FITTED WITH NINE ONE-NINTH AND FOUR ONE-FOURTH LENSES, BOTH OR EITHER OF THE SETS.

is our Success Camera, O, similar in style, though more elaborately finished. Being manufactured in mahogany, or hard-word ebonized, and provided with nickel trimmings, the latter are decidedly the best and most desirable cameras of the kind in the market. Negatives as well as ferrotypes can be made with either of them.

THE PUBLISHERS.

AUTHOR'S ADDENDA.

Each of the former editions of "The Ferrotype, and How to Make It," were ornamented with one or more samples of ferrotypes, which were intended to convey to the amateur, or prospective professional, an idea of the best that could be done with the materials provided for the purpose by the most prominent stock-house and manufacturers of photographic requisites in the country.

When it was decided to print a third edition, it was thought advisable to again send out with the book a specimen of the best work of the special branch of the art to which it was devoted, and it was also believed that such improvements as have been introduced of late years might in this manner be best illustrated and brought to the attention of the reader.

Messrs. E. & H. T. Anthony & Co., the present owners of the copyright, being desirous that the illustrations should be of the best, very kindly placed the resources of their immense establishment at my disposal, to select the materials from which to produce these pictures; and it is with no little pride I am able to state that, in tone, style, and finish, they excel any I have heretofore made for this purpose.

These points of excellence are partly attributable to the recent improvements in the materials, such as collodion, developer, silver solution, etc., and to the superiority of the instruments and apparatus.

The latter having been already described in a previous chapter, it is not necessary that further allusion should be made to them; suffice it to say, it is generally conceded that the Dallmeyer lenses and the Success Cameras lead the world.

Mention has also been made of the means for improving the tone of ferrotypes; these pictures, it is hoped, will demonstrate what can be done in that direction by the use of Tannic Acid in the developer, and of the Diamond Varnish in finishing.

A very large share of whatever excellence the pictures may possess is attributable to the uniform good qualities of the Adamantean Ferro-Plates of Messrs. John Dean & Co., upon which they were made. I have heretofore complimented them, and I only desire to say in this connection that these plates are made by workmen who know just what is wanted by the ferrotypist, and who also know how to make them, and they are made accordingly.

The abundance and great delicacy of detail result from E. & H. T. Anthony & Co's new and rapid collodions, the "New Negative" and "New Instantaneous." In connection with the H. T. A. developer, these collodions yield the most pleasing and satisfactory results.

E. M. ESTABROOKE.

ADDENDA.

To Remove Silver Stains.

The following mixture will remove all silver stains. Mix together and keep in a bottle:

Alcohol	20 parts.
Iodine	1 part.
Nitric acid	1 "
Hydrochloric acid	1 "

Apply this to the stain, and after a few minutes apply either a solution of hyposulphite of soda or of cyanide of potassium—the latter to be preferred. A second application is sometimes necessary. After the stain disappears wash well.

Thermometer Scales.

The zero of the Centigrade and of Reaumur's thermometor each correspond to 32° Fahrenheit.

To convert degrees of Reaumur into equivalent degrees of Fahrenheit, multiply the degrees of Reaumur by 9, divide the product by 4, and add 32; the result will be the degrees of Fahrenheit. 9 Fahrenheit, 5 Centigrade, and 4 Reaumur are equivalents. In Wedgwood's Pyrometer the zero commences at 1,077° Fahrenheit; and each degree, instead of being equal to 130° of Fahrenheit, as was supposed by its maker, is only equal to about 20°.

Easy Rules for the Reduction of Scales.

To convert Reaumur into Fahrenheit, multiply by 2.25 and add 32°.

To convert Centigrade into Fahrenheit, multiply by 1.8 and add 32°.

Sizes of Camera Plates.

Stereoscopic	5¼ by 3¼ inches, 6¾ by 3¼ inches.
9th Plate	2½ " 2 "
6th Plate	3¼ " 2¾ "
Quarter-Plate	4¼ " 3¼ "
One-third Plate	5 " 4 "
Half-Plate	6½ " 4¾ "
Whole Plate	8½ " 6½ "
Extra Sizes	10 by 8 inches, 12 " 10 "
	14 " 12 " 18 " 15 "
	24 " 18 " 30 " 26 "

TABLE FOR ENLARGEMENTS.

FOCUS OF LENS,	TIMES OF ENLARGEMENT AND REDUCTION.							
	1	2	3	4	5	6	7	8
inches.	inches.	inches.	inches.	inches.	inches.	inches.	inches.	inches.
2	4 4	6 3	8 2⅔	10 2½	12 2⅖	14 2⅓	16 2²⁄₇	18 2¼
2½	5 5	7½ 3¾	10 3⅓	12½ 3⅛	15 3	17½ 2 11/12	20 2⁶⁄₇	22½ 2 13/16
3	6 6	9 4½	12 4	15 3¾	18 3⅗	21 3½	24 3³⁄₇	27 3⅜
3½	7 7	10½ 5¼	14 4⅔	17½ 4⅜	21 4⅕	24½ 4 1/12	28 4	31½ 3 15/16
4	8 8	12 6	16 5⅓	20 5	24 4⅘	28 4⅔	32 4⁴⁄₇	36 4½
4½	9 9	13½ 6¾	18 6	22½ 5⅝	27 5⅖	31½ 5¼	36 5⅐	40½ 5 1/16
5	10 10	15 7½	20 6⅔	25 6¼	30 6	35 5⅚	40 5⁵⁄₇	45 5⅝
5½	11 11	16½ 8¼	22 7⅓	27½ 6⅞	33 6⅗	38½ 6 5/12	44 6²⁄₇	49½ 6 3/16
6	12 12	18 9	24 8	30 7½	36 7⅕	42 7	48 6⁶⁄₇	54 6¾
7	14 14	21 10½	28 9⅓	35 8¾	42 8⅖	49 8⅙	56 8	63 7⅞
8	16 16	24 12	32 10⅔	40 10	48 9⅗	56 9⅓	64 9⅐	72 9
9	18 18	27 13½	36 12	45 11¼	54 10⅘	63 10½	72 10²⁄₇	81 10⅛

THE object of this table is to enable any manipulator who is about to enlarge or reduce a copy any given number of times, to do so without troublesome calculation. It is assumed that the photographer knows exactly what the focus of his lens is, and that he is able to measure accurately from its optical center. The use of the table will be seen from the following illustration: A photographer has a carte to enlarge to four times its size, and the lens he intends employing is one of six inches equivalent focus. He must, therefore, look for 4 on the upper horizontal line, and for 6 in the first vertical column, and carry his eye to where these two join, which will be at 30—7½. The greater of these is the distance the sensitive plate must be from the center of the lens; and the lesser, the distance of the picture to be copied. To reduce a picture any given number of times, the same method must be followed, but in this case the greater number will represent the distance between the lens and the picture to be copied; the lesser, that between the lens and the sensitive plate. This explanation will be sufficient for every case of enlargement or reduction.

If the focus of the lens be 12 inches, as this number is not in our column of focal lengths, look out for 6 in this column and multiply by 2; and so on with any other numbers.

ADDENDA.

WEIGHTS AND MEASURES.

Troy, or Apothecaries' Weight.

1 pound = 12 ounces; 1 ounce = 8 drachms; 1 drachm = 3 scruples; 1 scruple = 20 grains. (1 ounce Troy = 480 grains, or 1 ounce Avoirdupois + 52·5 grains.)

Avoirdupois Weight.

1 pound = 16 ounces; 1 ounce = 16 drachms; 1 drachm = 27·348 grains. (1 ounce Avoirdupois = 437·5 grains. 1 pound Avoirdupois = 7000 grains, or 1 pound Troy + 2½ Troy ounces + 40 grains.)

Imperial Measure.

1 gallon = 8 pints; 1 pint = 20 ounces; 1 ounce = 8 drachms; 1 drachm = 60 minims. (A water-pint of water measures 16 ounces, and weighs a pound.)

An Imperial gallon of water *weighs* 10 pounds Avoirdupois, or 70,000 grains. An Imperial pint of water *weighs* 1¼ pound Avoirdupois. A fluid ounce of water *weighs* 1 ounce Avoirdupois, or 437·5 grains. A drachm of water *weighs* 54·7 grains.

French Measures of Weight.

1 kilogramme = 1000 grammes = something less than 2¼ pounds Avoirdupois.

1 gramme = 10 décigrammes = 100 centigrammes = 1000 milligrammes = 15·433 English grains.

A gramme of water *measures* 17 English minims, nearly. 1000 grammes of water *measure* 35¼ English fluid ounces.

French Measures of Volume.

1 litre = 10 décilitres = 100 centilitres = 1000 millitres = 35¼ English fluid ounces.

1 litre = 1 cubic décimètre = 1000 cubic centimètres.

1 cubic centimètre = 17 English minims.

A litre of water *weighs* a kilogramme, or something less than 2¼ pounds Avoirdupois. A cubic centimètre of water *weighs* a gramme.

WEIGHTS AND MEASURES.

APOTHECARIES' WEIGHT.—SOLID MEASURE.

20 grains	= 1 scruple =	20 grains.
3 scruples	= 1 drachm =	60 "
8 drachms	= 1 ounce =	480 "
12 ounces	= 1 pound =	5760 "

FLUID.   **SYMBOL.**

60 minims	= 1 fluid drachm.	f. ʒ
8 drachms	= 1 ounce.	f. ℥
20 ounces	= 1 pint.	O. ℥
8 pints	= 1 gallon.	gall.

The above weights are those usually adopted in formulæ. All Chemicals are usually sold by

AVOIRDUPOIS WEIGHT.

27 1/3 grains	= 1 drachm =	27 1/3 grains.
16 drachms	= 1 ounce =	437 1/2 "
16 ounces	= 1 pound =	7000 "

Precious Metals are usually sold by

TROY WEIGHT.

24 grains	= 1 pennyweight =	24 grains.
20 pennyweights	= 1 ounce	= 480 "
12 ounces	= 1 pound	= 5760 "

NOTE.—An ounce of *metallic* silver contains 480 grains, but an ounce of *nitrate* of silver contains only 437½ grains.

FRENCH WEIGHTS AND MEASURES,

AND THEIR EQUIVALENTS IN ENGLISH.

1 cubic centimetre	=	17 minims, nearly.
3½ " "	=	1 drachm.
28·4 " "	=	1 ounce.
50 " "	=	1 ounce 6 drachms 5 minims.
100 " "	=	3 ounces 4 drachms 9 minims.
1000 " " or 1 litre, = to 61 cubic inches.	=	35 ounces 1 drachm 36 minims.

The unit of French liquid measures is a cubic centimetre. A cubic centimetre of water measures nearly 17 minims (16·896); it weighs 15·4 grains, or 1 gramme. A cubic inch of water weighs 252·5 grains.

The unit of French weights is the gramme,—to 15·4 grains; thus a drachm (60 grains) is nearly 4 grammes (3·88). An easy way to convert grammes into English weight, is to divide the sum by 4, which gives the equivalent in drachms very nearly thus:

    GRAMMES.   DRACHMS.   OZ.   DRCHM.   GRAINS.
    100 ÷ 4 = 25 = 3 . 1 + 42.

THE END.

Enterprising Photographers,

desiring to keep fully acquainted with the latest improvements in methods and materials, subscribe to the leading American Photographic Journal,

ANTHONY'S
Photographic * Bulletin.

EDITORS: { PROF. CHAS. F. CHANDLER, PH.D., LL.D.,
FREDERICK J. HARRISON.

ISSUED MONTHLY.

An Actual Photograph in Every Issue.

PRACTICAL ARTICLES ON TOPICAL SUBJECTS.

SUBSCRIPTION RATES.

Per Year..$2.00
Per Copy... .25
Foreign, per year................................ 3.00

☞ Subscriptions to ANTHONY'S PHOTOGRAPHIC BULLETIN will be received by all Photographic Stock Dealers, by the American News Company, and by

E. & H. T. ANTHONY & CO.,
591 Broadway, New York.

ANTHONY'S
New Ferrotype Collodion,

Expressly for FERROTYPE WORK,

Is Unequaled by any in the Market.

ITS SALE IS CONSTANTLY INCREASING.

PUT UP IN HALF-POUND BOTTLES.

Price, per Pound, $1.20.

FOR SALE BY ALL DEALERS.

— MANUFACTURED BY —

E. & H. T. ANTHONY & CO.,

591 Broadway, New York.

ANTHONY'S
PURE CHEMICALS.

THE BRAND

E. A.

is a guarantee of the purity of the chemicals. Use only these and you will make sure of having only

THE BEST.

SOLUBLE COTTONS,
    CONC. SULPHURIC ETHER,
        IODIDE OF AMMONIUM,
            IODIDE OF CADMIUM,
                ANTHONY'S VARNISHES,
                    C. P. SULPHATE OF IRON,
                        PYROGALLIC ACID,
IODIZED COLLODIONS,
    ALCOHOL,
        BROMIDE OF AMMONIUM,
            BROMIDE OF CADMIUM,
                OXALATE OF POTASH,
                    CHLORIDE OF GOLD,
                        SULPHITE OF SODA.

Our Chemicals are endorsed by every Photographer of note in the United States.

E. & H. T. ANTHONY & CO.,
591 Broadway, New York.

5 x 7 IMPROVED VICTORIA CAMERA.

For making 5 x 7, 4½ x 5½ and 3¼ x 4¼ pictures, and reversible, and 4 or 8 on 5 x 7 plates with 4 Gem tubes. It is handsomely finished in mahogany, has rabbeted shield and kits. The camera has several improvements over anything heretofore offered to the trade.

Price, without lenses.................................$15 00
" with 4 ½ lenses on plate...................... 31 50

NEW YORK GEM CAMERA.

This Camera has been in great demand for small ferro. work and photographs to half size.

No. 42. For 4, 8 and 16 on 1-4 plate with 4 1-9 lenses 2 on 1-2 plate, and 1-2 to 1-6 reversible with 1 portrait lens—without lenses..$15 00
The same with lenses.. 24 00

E. & H. T. ANTHONY & CO., 591 Broadway, New York.

CLIMAX FERROTYPE CAMERAS.

	Without Lenses.	With Lenses.
No. 37½. Camera and shield for 4 on 1-4 plate with 4 1-9 lenses.......	$6 75	$16 00
No. 38. Camera and shield for 6 on 1-2 plate with 6 1-9 lenses.......	8 50	22 25
No. 39. Camera and shield for 9 on 5-7 plate with 9 1-9 lenses.......	12 00	32 50

No. 41. This is an excellent and cheap Camera for making four bon-tons on a 5 x 7 ferro-plate with four tubes, or one card or cabinet picture on a 5 x 7 plate with one lens.
Without lenses......................... $12 00
Fitted with four 1-4 lenses..................... 27 50

MANUFACTURED BY

E. & H. T. ANTHONY & CO.,

591 BROADWAY, NEW YORK.

Ferrotype Outfit No. 1.

For those who wish to start on a small scale, the following outfit will suffice for a beginning:

1 ¼ Gem Camera and Holders, with 4 1-9 Gem Lenses, to make 4 1-9 Gems on ¼ plate..................
1 Short Head Rest..................
1 ¼ Excel. Camera Stand..................
1 ¼ Rubber Bath and Dipper..................
1 4 x 5 Rubber Dish..................
2 No. 0 Rubber Funnels..................
1 3 oz. Collodion Vial..................
1 3 oz. Graduated Glass..................
1 Alcohol Lamp..................
1 Box Ferro. Colors, Brushes, etc..................
1 ½ Pint Jar Paste and Brush..................
1 Quill Duster..................
1 Instruction Book, The Ferrotype and How to Make It.....
1 Box ¼ Ferro. Plates..................
500 No. 4 Ferrotype Envelopes..................
1 Pint Silver Bath Solution..................
¼ lb. Ferrotype Collodion..................
1 lb. Acetic Acid..................
¼ lb. Cyanide Potassium..................
1 lb. Sulph. Iron, in bottle..................
1 Bottle Varnish..................
1 Pint 95° Alcohol..................

TOTAL..................$37 95

Those who wish to make single pictures, 1-9, 1-6 and 1-4 sizes, can do so with this outfit by adding a ¼ E. A. Portrait Lens, with central stops, which will cost, extra, $8.75.

The same outfit as above, but instead of ¼ Camera, Stand, Bath and Dish, we will send ½ sizes, $38.70.

With ¼ E. A. Lens..................$46 70
With 1-3 E. A. Lens.................. 52 50

MANUFACTURED BY

E. & H. T. ANTHONY & CO.,

591 Broadway, New York.

FERROTYPE OUTFIT No. 2.

The following outfit will be found the best for traveling business on a small scale:

- 1 1-2 Combination Camera makes 1-9, 1-6, 1-4 and 1-2 single Ferrotypes, and 2 card size on a ½ plate with 1 ½ size Lens. Price of Camera and E. A. Lens...
- 1 ½ Excel. Camera Stand.
- 1 Tall Head Rest........
- 1 ½ Glass Bath in Box, and Dipper..........
- 1 5 x 7 Rubber Dish......
- 1 Alcohol Lamp..........
- 1 4-oz. Collodion Vial.....
- 1 4-oz. Graduated Glass...
- 2 No. 1 Rubber Funnels..
- 1 Pint Silver Solution....
- 1 lb. Sulph. Iron, in bottle
- 1 lb. Acetic Acid, in bottle
- ½ lb. Cyanide Potassium.
- ¼ lb. Ferro. Collodion....
- 1 Bottle Varnish, Crystal..
- 1 Box Colors, Brushes and Gold Saucer..........
- 1 Pint 95° Alcohol........
- 1 Box each ¼ and ½ Ferrotype Plates..........
- 100 No. 11 Ferrotype Envelopes.............
- 50 No. 24 Card Envelopes.
- ½ Pint Jar Paste and Brush.............
- 1 1-inch Camel's Hair Duster for Plates.....
- 1 Copy Ferrotype and How to Make It.........

TOTAL..........$51 93

FERROTYPE OUTFIT No. 3.

For those who wish to make larger pictures, the following will be found a good outfit:

- 1 8 x 10 Cincinnati Gem Camera and Holder, carriage movement, fitted with 4 ¼ E. A. Lenses, plain..........
- 1 4-4 E. A. Portrait Lens, C. S.................
- 1 No. 2 Acme Camera Stand, boxed........
- 1 Tall Head Rest........
- 1 9 x 12 Glass Bath, in box, and Dipper..........
- 1 8 x 10 Rubber Dish.....
- 1 Alcohol Lamp..........
- 1 8-oz. Collodion Vial....
- 1 8-oz. Graduated Glass..
- 2 No. 3 Rubber Funnels..
- 1 Box Ferrotype Colors, Brushes, etc.........
- 3 Pints Silver Bath Solution
- 2 lbs. Acetic Acid........
- 1 lb. Sulph. Iron, in bottle
- 1 lb. Cyanide Potassium..
- 1 lb. Ferro. Collodion ...
- 1 Pint Ferro. Varnish. ...
- 1 Pint 95° Alcohol.......
- 1 ½ Pint Jar Paste and Brush.............
- 1 ½ inch Camel's Hair Duster..........
- 50 10 x 14 Ferro. Plates...
- 500 No. 11 Ferrotype Envelopes.............
- 100 No. 15 Ferrotype Envelopes for ½ size....
- 24 No. 20 Cabinet Envelopes
- 1 Copy Ferrotype and How to Make It.........

TOTAL..........$118 00

Those who do not care to make large pictures can dispense with the 4-4 Lens.

Or a ½ size E. A. Portrait Lens can be substituted for $17.50, making this outfit very useful.

NOTE.—To these outfits may be added other articles to make them more complete (but can be dispensed with, if economy is an object), such as Backgrounds and Accessories, Posing Chair, Tent, etc.

Manufactured by E. & H. T. ANTHONY & CO.,
591 Broadway, New York.

Climax Portrait and Gem Camera.
(No. 43 C.)

The best every-day Camera in the market. With sliding holder and swinging ground glass; improved focus screw; extension bellows. With rabbeted kits for dry-plate and ferrotype work. With a single 4-4 or extra 4-4 tube, it will make all regular work, reversible, from 1-4 size to 8 x 10; also two cabinets on 8 x 10 plate, or two 5 x 7 size on two 5 x 7 plates. With a 1-4 or 1-2 size tube, copying and enlarging to 8 x 10; with four 1-4 Gem tubes set in brass plate, it makes eight large bon-tons or card size on 7 x 10; also four of the same size on 5 x 7, and eight small bon-tons on 5 x 7. Prices:

No. 43 C. All complete except tubes............ $22 50
" 43 C. As above, fitted with four 1-4 Gem tubes, 37 50

MANUFACTURED BY

E. & H. T. ANTHONY & CO.,
591 BROADWAY, NEW YORK.

THE "BENSTER" PLATE HOLDER.

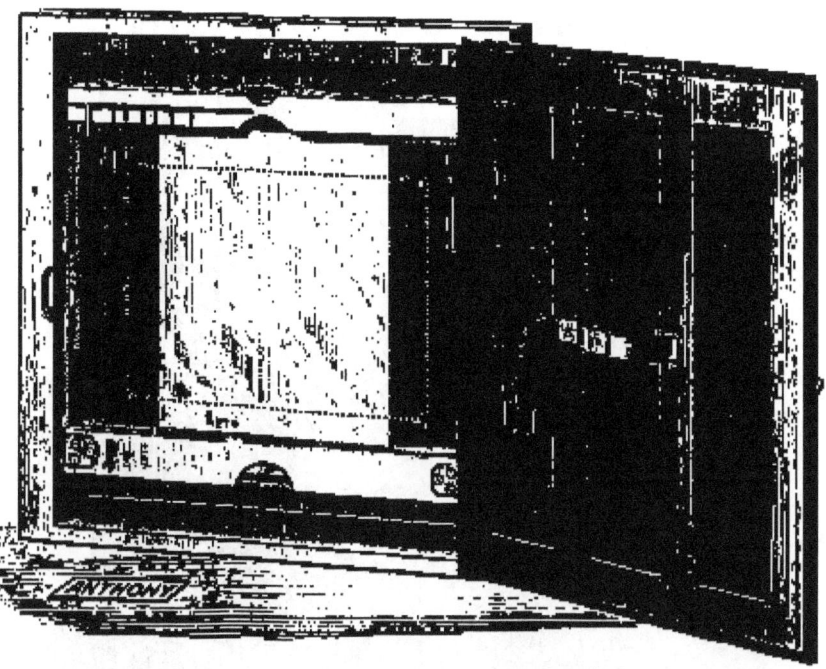

The plate rests on pure silver wire, and there is a trough, with large bottle beneath, into which all the silver waste readily finds its way. As the trough is raised, the upper ledge descends, so that the center of the plate is at all times in the center of the holder, no matter what size is used. This obviates the use of inside kits, and adapts itself at once to any size of plate, from the largest the holder will admit to one not under 3 inches square. This is unquestionably the best gallery plate holder made. By a recent improvement, the horizontal bars may be instantly fastened for plates of any size, and there is also an attachment for the vertical adjustment.

The prices of Benster Holders for Portrait Cameras are as follows:

For	8 x 10 plate and under,	12½ in. wide,	13⅜ in. high	$10 00
"	8 x 10	"	"	13¾	"	13¾	"	10 00
"	10 x 12	"	"	15	"	15¾	"	14 00
"	11 x 14	"	"	17	"	17¾	"	18 00
"	14 x 17	"	"	20½	"	21	"	22 00
"	17 x 20	"	"	23½	"	24	"	25 00
"	20 x 24	"	"	28	"	28½	"	35 00
"	22 x 27	"	"	31	"	31½	"	40 00

Special sizes to order, will cost 20 per cent. additional.

Manufactured by E. & H. T. ANTHONY & CO.,

591 Broadway, New York.

CLIMAX CINCINNATI GEM CAMERA.

FITTED WITH THE "BENSTER" PLATE HOLDER.

For negatives or ferrotypes (admitting of picture 8 x 10 and under, two on 8 x 10, 7 x 10, or 5 x 7 with one lens), with carriage movement on our Patent Rollers, and fitted with the "Benster" Holder.

No.		Price.
43 B.	Without swing	$27 00
43 B.	Single swing	30 00
43 B.	Double swing	34 50

When fitted with four 1-4 Gem Tubes on plate, it will admit of eight on 7 x 10, and four on 5 x 7.

		Price.
Without swing, fitted with four tubes on plate		$43 00
Single " " " " "		46 00
Double " " " " "		50 00

MANUFACTURED BY

E. & H. T. ANTHONY & CO.,

591 Broadway, New York.

ANTHONY'S "GIANT" CAMERA STAND.

Without any exceptions the Best ever made.

STRONG! RIGID! DURABLE! CHEAP!

Goes lower than any other.   Minimum height, 19 inches.

THE SIMPLEST STAND ON THE MARKET.

The least mechanism.   No weights.

PRICES.

8 x 10 to 11 x 14, ... $16 50

E. & H. T. ANTHONY & CO.,
591 Broadway, New York.

THE KNICKERBOCKER STAND.

THE ACME TOP.

Each stand is packed in a separate box. The tops are attached to the upright with screws, in metallic ears, and the legs are firmly fastened with screws to the center-piece, and are removed when packed. The tops of Nos. 1, 2, 3 and 4 are elevated by means of a snake screw operating on a cog-wheel, and this in turn on the metallic rack of the standard or upright. This peculiar arrangement greatly diminishes the friction, and therefore very little power suffices in elevating or lowering the camera. The tops of Nos. 0 and 1 are inclined by means of a cam operated by a snake screw, while that of No. 4 is after Stoddard's pattern. We annex a cut of No. 4 entire. Nos. 2 and 3 have the Acme top.

WITH KNICKERBOCKER TOP.
No. 0, for 4-4 Camera.... $5 00
" 1, " " " 6 25

WITH ACME TOP.
No. 2, for 8 x 10 Camera... $9 00
" 3, " " " ...10 50

No. 4, for 8 x 10 Camera, with Stoddard top....$13 50

Manufactured by E. & H. T. ANTHONY & CO.,
591 Broadway, New York.

IRON CENTER STAND.

This is now the favorite cheap stand. Being in walnut, and the iron center bronzed, its general appearance is quite pleasing.

Price, for 1-4, 1-2, 4-4 and 8 x 10..................$3 50

THE LEVER STAND.

Suited to all sizes from 8 x 10 to 14 x 17. Price, $12 00

MANUFACTURED BY

E. & H. T. ANTHONY & CO.,

591 Broadway, New York.

Photographic Card and Ferrotype Plate Cutter.

Photographers will find this a grand thing for cutting albumen paper, and it is also invaluable for cutting ferrotype plates.

The advantages of this cutter are: with 12-inch blades it will cut any size sheet. No other machine ever made will cut a sheet wider than the length of the blades.

All the parts are made to gauges, by which they are interchangeable, so that if any part is worn out, broken or lost, a duplicate can be ordered.

All the parts are made of the best material, and a cutter capable of a range of work never before attempted in a small machine is offered at less than one-half the price of any other cutter with same length of blades.

Price, only $10.00 for a complete machine, with adjustable gauges and latest improvements. Each machine boxed, and no extra charges.

Directions for Using the Premium Card Cutter.

Attach the gauge-bar to the under side of the bed near the front edge by three screws, which will be found in place. See that the small rubber stop for the blade is inserted in the hole in the front of bed before screwing the gauge permanently to place. It will always be found in the proper place, unless it has been accidentally removed. The pin through the square part of the bolt is to be placed in the slot in bar, to positively avoid the turning of the bolt. To attach the gauge to the gauge-bar, remove the bolt from the gauge, and passing the bolt up through the slot in the gauge-bar attach the gauge as shown in cut.

FOR SALE BY

E. & H. T. ANTHONY & CO.,
591 Broadway, New York.

Adamantean Ferrotype Plates.

					Eggshell.	Glossy.
Box of 8 dozen,	Black or Chocolate Tint,	1-9 Size	....	$0 80	$0 90
" 8	"	"	1-6 "	....	1 25	1 35
" 8	"	"	1-4 "	....	1 85	2 00
" 4	"	"	1-2 "	....	2 20	2 35
" 4	"	"	4¼ x 6½ Size,	2 20	2 35
" 4	"	"	5 x 7	"	2 40	2 70
" 2	"	"	6½ x 8½	"	2 40	2 70
" 2	"	"	7 x 10	"	2 70	2 90
200 Sheets	"	"	10 x 14	"	28 00	30 00

The best and most uniform plates in the market.

Ferrotype Plates.

EUREKA—Box of 200 10 x 14 Egg-shell,
  Black or Chocolate.........$20 00... Glossy....$22 00
UNION—Box of 200 10 x 14 Egg-shell,
  Black or Chocolate......... 15 00....Per dozen, 90

FOR SALE BY

E. & H. T. Anthony & Co.,

591 Broadway, New York.

5/8 FIVE-EIGHTHS

of the entire amount of Paper consumed in the United States, is American "Aristo."—Ninety Percent of the Leading Photographers use it exclusively.

WHY?

| Captured ONLY award on printing-out papers at the World's Fair. | Captured Eleven out of Fifteen Prizes at P. A. of A. Convention, July, 1893. |

MANUFACTURERS:
AMERICAN ARISTOTYPE CO.,
JAMESTOWN, N. Y.

SOLE AGENTS:
E. & H. T. ANTHONY & CO.,
591 BROADWAY, NEW YORK.

www.ingramcontent.com/pod-product-compliance
Lightning Source LLC
Chambersburg PA
CBHW020848160426
43192CB00007B/830